Intelligent Disobedience

Obeying all of the rules rarely generates breakthrough business performance because it does not generate new approaches. Breaking the rules randomly does not work either. Intelligent disobedience values improved business performance over compliance with the rules, when conditions permit. This is the essence of intelligent disobedience: knowing when and how to break, bend, or invent new rules to get better outcomes.

This book promotes enhanced performance by promoting a higher form of ethics. Intelligent disobedience seeks to surface hidden truth and to produce actions that are of higher integrity to yield superior results. The book guides the reader to evaluate their work environment, current business results, and risk, to determine when acting with intelligent disobedience can enhance their business outcomes and their career.

Intelligent Disobedience: The Difference between Good and Great Leaders seeks to:

- enhance the reader's business success;
- help the reader to examine methods for proposing potentially unpopular directions or opinions;
- propose a decision-making process for when the reader should "bend or break the rules" – leveraging common sense over common processes on an exception basis;
- guide the reader to determine instances in which improved outcomes are better than ensuring compliance with corporate norms or management directions.

This rich and sophisticated book interweaves real-life experiences from successful leaders with the themes of human psychology, ethics, decision making, delegation, communicating upwards and downwards . . . Everything the senior manager needs to survive and thrive in a complex, uncertain, ambiguous, and fast-changing world.

Bob McGannon is director of Intelligent Disobedience Leadership, and has worked in management roles in the United States, Europe, and Australia. Over a career spanning 35 years, Bob has managed technology teams, outsourced services, and major change initiatives for large companies. He is also an entrepreneur, having launched and directed three companies in the consulting and training industries.

Bob is an author of more than 20 courses that can be found on the online LinkedIn Learning platform and has contributed chapters to two compiled works: *Advising Upwards*, edited by Linda Bourne; and *The Keys to Our Success: Lessons Learned from 25 of Our Best Project Managers*, edited by David Barrett. In addition, Bob has written numerous articles for his company newsletters and writes the Intelligent Disobedience blog (http://www.intelligentdisobedience.com).

Bob's passions are developing people, team creation, motivation and management focused on strategic implementation, and day-to-day process optimization. He is known for building cohesive, high-performing teams through strategy, culture development, project management, and suitable doses of intelligent disobedience – with a bit of fun mixed in.

Bob is married, with one daughter, a grand-cat, a grand-dog, and a grand-lizard, and he splits his time between Queensland, Australia, and Minnesota, USA.

Intelligent Disobedience

The Difference between Good and Great Leaders

Bob McGannon

 Routledge
Taylor & Francis Group

LONDON AND NEW YORK

First published 2018
by Routledge
2 Park Square, Milton Park, Abingdon, Oxon OX14 4RN

and by Routledge
711 Third Avenue, New York, NY 10017

Routledge is an imprint of the Taylor & Francis Group, an informa business

British Library Cataloguing-in-Publication Data
A catalogue record for this book is available from the British Library

Library of Congress Cataloging-in-Publication Data
Names: McGannon, Bob, 1960- author.
Title: Intelligent disobedience : the difference between good and
    great leaders / Bob McGannon.
Description: Abingdon, Oxon ; New York, NY : Routledge, 2018. |
    Includes bibliographical references and index. |
Identifiers: LCCN 2017050234 (print) | LCCN 2017054516 (ebook)
    | ISBN 9781315178417 (eBook) | ISBN 9781138036512
    (hardback : alk. paper) | ISBN 9780815394679 (pbk : alk. paper)
Subjects: LCSH: Leadership. | Executives. | Performance.
Classification: LCC HD57.7 (ebook) | LCC HD57.7 .M39558 2018
    (print) | DDC 658.4/092—dc23
LC record available at https://lccn.loc.gov/2017050234

ISBN: 9781138036512 (hbk)
ISBN: 9780815394679 (pbk)
ISBN: 9781315178417 (ebk)

Typeset in Times New Roman
by Swales & Willis Ltd, Exeter, Devon, UK

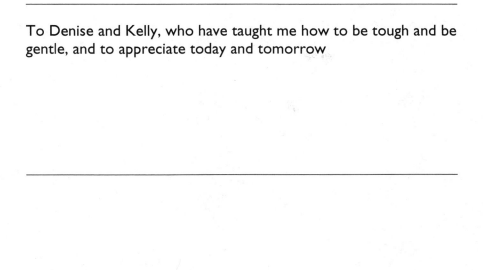

To Denise and Kelly, who have taught me how to be tough and be gentle, and to appreciate today and tomorrow

Contents

Figures

Tables

Acknowledgements

I feel tremendous gratitude to the leaders who showed me examples of intelligent disobedience and how it makes a difference, the managers who supported my intelligent disobedience, and the teams I worked with who did not lose faith while I experimented with intelligent disobedience. I know that my teams were sometimes unsure about my intelligent disobedience approach . . . Thanks for hanging in there with me and sharing in the improved results.

I'm also grateful to the leaders who challenged or opposed my intelligent disobedience. They helped me to define boundaries, understand different corporate standards and contexts, and expand my views on the homework required to perform intelligent disobedience.

I want to thank Bonnie Biafore, who believed in this book years before it was written. Her skills at organizing my thoughts, her patient and fierce editing, and her sense of humor were instrumental to this book being in your hands.

Jonathan Norman from Taylor & Francis was another believer in the potential of this book. His support and gentle guidance were instrumental. Thank you, kind sir! Kudos also to Vanessa Plaister, Adam Guppy and Tom Cole for your work and constant professionalism. Special thanks to Alex Atkinson who endured my endless questions and pestering with patience and kindness.

This book would not be pragmatic without the support of the people who shared their stories, fears, and motivations. Every day, each of them seeks to learn and teach. They represent the best leaders I have encountered. I hope this book expands the support they receive, because their insights have literally saved organizations from themselves! You are all awesome.

I would not be the person or author I am without the support of Denise, my wife, business partner, travel buddy, and best friend. You are my world. My daughter Kelly deserves recognition as well. She constantly reminds me not to take myself too seriously and to enjoy the moment. The friends who have supported this work are extensive. Special thanks to Jade, Nic, Doris, Dr. Linda, and Donna, who took the time to read the drafts of this book and support this journey. You're the best!

Lastly, I want to thank the attendees of my keynote speeches and intelligent disobedience workshops, who have freely shared anecdotes and experiences. Their tales have been invaluable, validating and refining the recommendations, ethical views, and approaches I describe in this book.

Introduction

My perspective on leadership changed in a hotel lobby in San José, California. I was alone, waiting for the elevator to whisk me to my room after an unusually long workday. A gentleman with a seeing-eye guide dog walked up and joined the wait.

That was when something extraordinary happened.

An elevator car reached the lobby. A chime announced its arrival, and the doors whooshed open. But the elevator had not landed correctly. The car had stopped about 8 inches below the floor level: an unexpected and potentially hazardous drop for someone entering the elevator. At the same time, what had been a calm and docile guide dog leapt – literally – into action. The seeing-eye dog jumped forward and turned his body 90 degrees, creating a barrier between his master and the hazardous elevator car.

I told my fellow elevator rider what had happened to the elevator and described the extraordinary act his dog had just performed. He said that type of action is categorized as *intelligent disobedience*.

"I give my dog Chap commands all the time," he said, "and he faithfully responds. On occasion, however, he doesn't obey my commands – or even gives commands of his own, as you saw here. I have to tell Chap what I want to do, and, at the same time, I put our safety in his hands. When he disobeys, I obey him!"

I found it interesting that, in this situation, the faithful Chap had not only disobeyed, but also literally presented a hurdle to what his master sought to accomplish.

From that evening forward, I considered the most effective leadership in the context of intelligent disobedience.

This book explores various techniques for engaging in intelligent disobedience. It also provides guidance on the types of information you need to assess whether an act of intelligent disobedience will be perceived in a positive light. You will also learn when intelligent disobedience is not a good idea.

My intent is to help you to explore intelligent disobedience, while providing tips, techniques, and tools for successfully incorporating intelligent disobedience into your business approach. I have made recommendations on how to design acts of intelligent disobedience and how to conduct "research homework" to help to increase the probability that your acts of intelligent disobedience will be perceived positively. In addition, I've provided techniques for determining whether intelligently disobedient actions could be viable or should be avoided.

Take or leave things as you see fit. Weigh your own appetite for risk, and consider whether your position on certain risks appropriately serves you and your business.

Chapter I

What is intelligent disobedience?

In the business context, intelligent disobedience is an act performed with the intent to create a better outcome than would be achieved by following standard rules, practices, or current management direction. Intelligent disobedience means valuing outcomes over compliance with existing guidelines and processes, when circumstances permit.

Under normal circumstances, we, as leaders or employees, should do as we are instructed – following standard procedures and working within the parameters of our job descriptions. However, in some circumstances, those rules and processes do not serve our organization's interests or may create detrimental outcomes for the managers who've provided the guidance. In these instances, the best leaders I've worked with turn to acts of intelligent disobedience. They evaluate whether bending (or breaking) a rule or countering a direction given by management would "protect their business," achieve a more favorable outcome, or avoid a harmful result.

Intelligent disobedience from different viewpoints

Anyone in an organization can engage in intelligent disobedience. In fact, for the best results, many people in an organization should be empowered to consider employing intelligent disobedience.

Empowering people in this way should not be done in a haphazard manner. The stakes of breaking or bending the rules can be high, so care should be taken to define appropriate limits or boundaries before allowing people to perform acts of intelligent disobedience. Without those limits or careful consideration of circumstances, acts of intelligent disobedience could suffer from an acute shortage of "intelligence."

It would, for example, be inappropriate to commit an act of intelligent disobedience that directly violates the law. Purposefully scheduling an airline pilot to violate their regulated rest periods for the time they fly an aircraft might result in a short-term cost reduction – but the safety risks to passengers and potential penalties imposed by a regulatory body easily offset any benefit. Add the effect of diminished public opinion from the perception of compromised safety and the result could be catastrophic to the business.

Given the potential for unintended results, an organization needs to take care and provide guidance to properly instill and manage the concept of intelligent disobedience. Every organization has its unique perspectives, which in turn determine which intelligent disobedience techniques are effective. For example, what may be considered intelligent disobedience within one organization may be commonplace at another. Reporting a minor personnel conflict to the HR director may be standard practice in some organizations, while others would expect the first-line management team to handle the issue.

Let's examine intelligent disobedience in different contexts: the first-line manager, the middle manager, and, finally, senior management.

Intelligent disobedience for first-line managers

In my experience, first-line managers, project managers, and team leaders perform most acts of intelligent disobedience. Typically, they do so when they feel empowered to manage their "piece of the business." They take the risks associated with bending the rules when they see the potential for a better outcome. Properly empowered individuals engage in intelligent disobedience within limits, where those limits are either assumed or defined over time and experience of working with their managers – the middle managers in the organization. Their intelligent disobedience can be a powerful factor in driving success.

First-line or project managers can enhance that power by intentionally acting to empower their staff. If a first-line manager's people are confident they can act with intelligent disobedience, similar to the way in which their manager does, performance improvement can be significant. Doing so mindfully is critical, however, because boundary conditions must be universally understood.

Defining the boundaries within which the manager's staff may act expands the organization's ability to produce optimal outcomes. Clearly stated boundaries help employees to feel confident that their acts of intelligent disobedience will be received appropriately.

Consider this example of clearly stated boundaries. I once worked with a logistics manager who elegantly directed his team to manage supplies across numerous groups with these intelligent disobedience guidelines:

1   Do not take action as a means of self-promotion. The overall organization must benefit from your actions.
2   Do not shift supplies to benefit one group at the expense of another.
3   Do not break the laws of our country and state.
4   Do not exceed budget limitations by greater than 5% for any given part number.
5   If you see an opportunity that will increase the effectiveness of the organization that does not follow standard practice, and that action does not violate guidelines 1 through 4, then feel free to act.

Having these guidelines is not enough, however; it is also critical to follow up after your team members have acted with intelligent disobedience. Timely follow-up provides encouragement. Notable acts of intelligent disobedience that are deployed successfully can also be rewarded. In addition, refining guidelines and continuously improving a team's approach to managing work helps the team to increase their performance. That results in overall improvement to the guidelines and processes used to manage intelligent disobedience, and in continued performance improvement.

When first-line managers actively and repeatedly discuss intelligent disobedience guidelines, their confidence to act grows. Particularly when intelligent disobedience requires a split-second decision, such as answering a challenging client question, a manager who confidently recalls a guideline discussion is much more likely to engage in an appropriate act of intelligent disobedience. Feedback collected from eight years of intelligent disobedience workshops shows that discussing guidelines greatly enhances the frequency and accuracy of how intelligent disobedience is employed. In addition, the results improve, because the management team more frequently supports the intelligent disobedience actions.

Intelligent disobedience at the middle-management level

While discussing parameters and constraints for acts of intelligent disobedience enhances the first-line manager's effectiveness, middle managers must embrace additional considerations to increase the power of intelligent disobedience in their organizations. From their positions of greater scope and breadth of responsibilities, middle managers who perform their own intelligent disobedient actions can more substantially affect the direction of the business. Middle managers who do this most effectively use the "eyes and ears" of their first-line managers and staff members, who can provide insights that might not be easily visible otherwise. Embracing the concept of intelligent disobedience typically increases the "rule-breaking" ideas that surface in management discussions, increasing possibilities for broader acts of intelligent disobedience. These actions can come with greater risks, however, because the visibility and scrutiny of intelligent disobedience actions taken by middle managers can affect organizational perceptions.

Middle management case study

Steve,[1] a middle manager in the medical instruments industry, was managing a geographically diverse set of support centers. His organization spent significant funds defining enhanced business processes and deploying a new computer system to support those processes. The usual bumps and small errors surfaced after implementation. However, capturing customer concerns for one line of medical devices was taking too long, and customers were reporting interpretation errors when the company tried to correct its devices.

Being in a highly regulated medical instruments industry, the company's corporate culture embraced processes and checklists, which were changed only after careful deliberation. Steve was a strong advocate of improved and unified processes, and repeatedly professed his belief in following new processes for an extended period before making changes. By not making changes too early, teams would not be tempted to revert to their old habits and processes.

Yet the high frequency of customer issues being reported from multiple geographies was a concern. Steve needed his team to perform well and to ensure that they addressed issues with the medical devices they supported.

Steve was faced with a difficult decision. Should he raise questions about the new support process, risk being perceived as a hypocrite, and potentially risk a cascade of nonoptimal process changes across the organization? Or should he ask his teams to continue to use the problematic processes, running the risk that the organization's performance would suffer?

Despite his concerns about downstream issues, Steve made a decision quickly: he had to put his customers first. A couple of his teams suggested an alternative process. The teams didn't collaborate, but the process change they proposed was strikingly similar. He brought members of those teams together and drafted a revised process that did not require an immediate change to their new system. Before deploying the change, he consulted with his management peers and shared his business problem, the analysis they undertook to improve the business process, his rationale for contradicting himself, and the direction he promoted for the organization. He conveyed this information using these simple steps.

1   Steve's team discovered a customer issue, rather than an issue of process comfort or familiarity for his staff, which changed his thinking about altering the new processes.

2   They worked hard to ensure that they were executing the process correctly before proposing a change.

3   Representatives of multiple teams who were having the same difficulty were instructed to collaborate to develop the change.

4   The new process design and evaluation sessions were recorded and made available on the company intranet, so that anyone could see how they analyzed the issue and solution.

5   Steve scheduled morning coffee breaks for teams within and outside of his organization because they might be aggravated by his "change of direction for self-centered reasons." He had a bakery make a cake in the shape of a crow – and he was filmed at the coffee breaks "eating crow" for changing his position so drastically.

In this example, Steve engaged in a significant act of intelligent disobedience by reversing his position and not enforcing the duration of time normally given to executing and validating processes in his organization. Steve made a bold move by admitting his need to change direction, publicizing the change, and taking steps in a time frame counter to that which would normally have been deemed acceptable. He maintained his integrity within the company and enhanced the effectiveness of this intelligent disobedience by turning his action into an organizational learning moment. He leveraged his role as a middle manager and the broad exposure it provided to set an example for those willing to follow. In addition, the "eating crow" gesture was a lighthearted way of getting people's attention and showing them that he was human, could make mistakes, and could admit them to the benefit of his organization.

Senior managers' perspective: directing middle managers

Ira Chaleff, author of *The Courageous Follower: Standing up to and for Our Leaders*,[2] has said that acts of intelligent disobedience can be the CEO's best friend. Similar to the interactions between lower levels of management, senior managers need to discuss acceptable boundaries and constraints to ensure that they embrace intelligent disobedience in a way deemed acceptable by the CEO and in line with the strategic vision and priorities of the business.

Senior leaders should consider an additional perspective of intelligent disobedience, over and above providing boundaries to the middle managers they lead. Understanding the goals, personality, strengths, and weaknesses of their middle managers is critical to appropriately managing the concept of intelligent disobedience. Some managers will have a difficult time altering culture, while building and maintaining culture may form the lifeblood of the success of others.

Some managers may have spent major portions of their career evolving products and services from existing offerings, or have worked in an entrepreneurial space in the past and be quite comfortable with new, innovative development. Each middle manager may have a different comfort level and willingness to engage in intelligent disobedience, and each may want to use different types of intelligent disobedience.

Wise senior leaders might choose not to encourage their entrepreneur-style middle managers to pursue changes to processes in a government-regulated business area, because those entrepreneurs may go too far or feel overly constrained to be successful. On the other hand, a process-minded middle manager may get bogged down in detail and lose the big picture when developing a new business concept where there are no rules.

Managing intelligent disobedience depends on understanding personalities and strengths. Therefore, to maximize the effectiveness of intelligent disobedience, senior managers must tune the constraints and boundaries for intelligent disobedience to suit each individual.

Effective intelligent disobedience involves balancing risks

Intelligent disobedience is not for the meek.

The very nature of intelligent disobedience involves engaging in actions that are not commonplace. Bending or breaking commonly held rules or norms, varying from supervisors' directions, discussing topics that are considered taboo, and so on, involve a degree of risk. You need to evaluate that risk compared to the potential benefits for your business, team, and the outcomes you are expected to deliver. Opportunities may be rich, but may be accompanied by ramifications of altered perceptions and concerns of those uncomfortable with straying from the status quo. Understanding and weighing the risks of intelligent disobedience is a crucial activity – and neglecting to do so may easily remove the "intelligence" from your attempt to engage in performance improvement.

This book frequently examines risks and how to evaluate them. This section reviews the most common risks you'll need to analyze when considering acts of intelligent disobedience.

Personal risks versus professional risks

Most people work to maintain their standard of living. Ideally, working is also an enjoyable experience. Whether or not that is the case, being pushed to change jobs or being perceived negatively in your current role can be extraordinarily uncomfortable. The most pressing (and sometimes desperate) question people ask, when discussing acts of intelligent disobedience, is: "What is the risk of being fired if I disobey my manager's direction?"

In some cases, the risk of being fired may exist – and, in some cases, being fired may be appropriate! However, when examining this risk in depth, its probability often turns out to be exaggerated. For instance, when a business outcome would plainly be improved, the risk of disciplinary action such as being fired is likely to be low.

People who are financially secure, are ambitious to achieve business success through improved performance, and are willing to take risks to succeed are more likely to take on the risks associated with intelligent disobedience. They are willing to risk some personal hardship in exchange for professional gain resulting from improved results.

Others without that level of financial comfort might resist acting with intelligent disobedience – but people in this category need to consider that doing nothing can also pose significant risk.

Risks now versus risks later

In weighing the risks of intelligent disobedience, we must consider what outcomes a given act of intelligent disobedience produces *now* versus the effect of suboptimal business results that come *later*.

Consider an example that illustrates *now versus later* risk.

Carla is an account manager responsible for technical equipment sales for a major company. The company's stubborn, marketing-driven manager directs her to follow a specific set of sales approaches and to pitch a particular set of products and associated features to her client. Carla feels strongly that the approach will not only fail, but could even alienate her client. Carla has a long-standing and successful relationship with her client, so she is troubled by the mandate to follow this sales approach.

Carla conveys her "now-focused" risk in this way.

- If I decide not to follow the mandated sales approach, I risk seriously aggravating the marketing manager. He has a very positive record and positional and political power in the organization. Therefore, not following his direction could put my job – which I thoroughly enjoy – in serious jeopardy.
- If I do use his sales model with my client, I risk harming my reputation as their pragmatic partner. I fear they will see my sales presentations as an insensitive quest for profit. This could reduce my chances of success when I see a legitimate need for our products. The client might not trust a future presentation, even though it's in their best interest, because of the harm this current sales approach does to my reputation.

Of greater concern to Carla are the "later-focused" risks of this situation. She describes them in this way.

- If I don't follow the sales direction I'm being given, I may experience a reduced reputation as a team player in my company. That could mean losing future opportunities as we expand our product line and client set.
- If I do follow the sales approach, my reputation may be diminished because my client loses trust and confidence in me. I will probably start missing my revenue targets. Because I handle a top-tier client of our company, missing revenue targets will lead to fewer opportunities for me.
- This new sales program represents a significant dilemma for me.

This is a poignant example of a "now versus later" risk profile. Avoiding an act of intelligent disobedience might seem like a safer path, but that safety can be fleeting – and it might simply delay the negative outcomes that only an act of intelligent disobedience could avoid.

What Carla did to address her dilemma is presented later.

Effectiveness versus image risks

Carla's dilemma presents risks to her image within her company and with her significant client. Image plays a role in another type of risk associated with intelligent disobedience: when taking the "right" or most effective action can diminish your reputation.

Suppose you are managing a project that is proceeding according to plan, and you present a relatively rosy picture of project status to senior management. At the status meeting, an executive asks if you foresee any major incidents occurring in the near future that could change this favorable status. Based on what your team has shared with you and your own intuition, you say you expect smooth sailing. The management team tells you that they are facing a substantial financial decision on another initiative. However, they would delay that initiative to ensure that resources were available for your project if it were having difficulties.

A couple of weeks later, the management team has launched the new initiative they discussed. One of your senior team members gives you very distressing news: they've been having trouble with a new component they are designing for your project. The issue's been going on for about three weeks. He and his team members were very confident they fully understood the cause of the problem and could fix it. Although the design and testing of the revised approach was going to take more than two weeks, they were so confident they had the solution that they didn't tell you about the issue. Now, they have to backtrack, which means expensive revisions to parts your company is purchasing and that more experienced resources from within your company are required to integrate those parts.

You know you need to communicate with your management team immediately. At the same time, doing so risks your image as a project manager who knows what's going on in your projects and controls project issues well.

Results versus compliance risks

Whether you manage a small organization or a large one, putting processes in place creates consistency and predictability when working with your customers, vendors, and colleagues. This consistency is designed to increase productivity and enables the continuous improvement that's almost mandatory for survival in today's business environment. However, organizational processes are drafted with knowledge of what is happening today and in anticipation of what is required for the future. Unusual situations, customers driving their own innovative changes, and competitive environments create circumstances in which your processes will not support desired outcomes.

I was managing the delivery of services for an IT outsourcing contract when an example of this risk became evident. Service-level agreements are at the core of outsourcing contracts; they define the essential elements and performance requirements for the customer. More stringent service levels may drive a higher quality service, but typically come with a higher price tag. An appropriate balance – anticipating current and future needs – is the hallmark of a sound set of service levels.

My outsourced-services client not only required high availability services, but also needed very consistent availability of service. If their IT services were available 99.9 percent of the time, but they had multiple outages of a few seconds each, they would feel a notable impact. They put service levels in place to address overall availability of their IT services and a target for the number of outages over a period of time, regardless of duration.

This contract structure served my client well until they decided to quickly add a new IT service to their portfolio to beat a competitor to the marketplace. Because this new technology product required interfaces to existing services, the risk of outages was significant while the new service was being implemented via numerous change events.

My services delivery team and I were faced with a choice: meet the contract parameters for the number of outages by restricting the work we did on the new service, or drive ahead to help our client to implement the new technology earlier. We could have easily referred to the service-level agreement and tailored our activity around those constraints. This would have assured that we maintained the stability the overall business needed, but would have increased risk for our client, who required quick implementation to stay competitive. By following our procedures and avoiding business issues, our reputation would remain intact.

We had to choose between complying with our processes to satisfy the agreement and changing our processes to help a subset of our client's business. In other words, we had to balance better long-term results for our client against following our procedures.

The intelligently disobedient solution we chose was to ask for a partial suspension of service levels for areas in which we thought outages presented the least risk to the business. This may seem obvious, but it triggered a political firestorm. Some areas of the business had no motivation to approve the partial suspension of the service levels; they didn't want changes implemented for what they considered a rogue business venture.

With the partial suspension of service levels we proposed, an outage caused by trying to bring the new service online would not incur a penalty unless the outage exceeded a specific duration. In this way, we dropped some elements of our compliance model so that we could improve the pathway to get the new service online quickly. This approach was accepted, and the new service was delivered in a timely fashion – but only after considerable senior manager intervention and assurances were provided.

To summarize, the desired result was achieved, but our act of intelligent disobedience required effort to defend, which is not uncommon in business areas in which management is siloed or significant reputational impacts could arise. You should carefully assess this type of risk.

Short-term versus long-term business impacts risks

Not all choices around engaging in intelligent disobedience have significant, uncontrolled risk; some are smaller, more pedestrian, issues. Nonetheless, acts of intelligent disobedience may be undertaken to achieve performance improvement. The most common examples I've heard from managers attending my intelligent disobedience workshops include the following.

- *Significant delegation* This represents delegating a notable task that stretches a staff member's capabilities. The positive outcome relates to the loyalty and abilities of your staff. The short-term risk relates to dealing with the issues that result from team members making mistakes that impact the business.
- *Letting something fail to drive learning* This activity reminds me of raising my daughter: sometimes, she needed to learn the pain of bad outcomes for

herself, rather than to listen to her dad. Similarly, strongly driven (and valuable) staff members and headstrong managers sometimes have to learn in a similar fashion by experiencing a less-than-optimal short-term outcome. The manager considering an act of intelligent disobedience here needs to assess the benefit of people's long-term learning versus the short-term implications of a suboptimal outcome.

- *Taking longer to achieve results in order to expand capabilities* A number of our clients have shared stories of instances in which they took the "long way" to achieve a result, as a means of expanding their team's capabilities. For example, rather than hiring a vendor to build a product, you may hire that same vendor to come into your organization and train your staff to build that product. This can take longer and cost more in the short term, but can reap long-term benefits in terms of the capability uplift experienced in the organization.

Intelligent disobedience and personal integrity

It's important to understand that intelligent disobedience does not advocate promoting a falsehood, compromising your own or other's integrity, or deceiving others in any way. If you believe that acts of intelligent disobedience violate these concepts, explore other options. Making this assessment can be a nontrivial act, however.

> 66 *It's important to understand that intelligent disobedience does not advocate promoting a falsehood, compromising your own or other's integrity, or deceiving others in any way.* 99

From the risks and actions described in the previous section, you might conclude that intelligent disobedience means compromising integrity. After all, would allowing an activity to fail represent something less than a high moral standard? (Chapter 3 talks about the ethical standing of intelligent disobedience.)

The following are some assessment items to help you to evaluate the integrity of an act of intelligent disobedience.

- Intelligent disobedience is *not* performing acts that benefit an individual rather than the business. Intelligent disobedience isn't about individual promotion; it is employed to deliver benefits to the business.
- Intelligent disobedience is *not* violating process or taking other unusual actions in relation to the law. You may be directed to refrain from acts of intelligent disobedience under any circumstances, for example where processes are in

place to comply with government regulation. Disobedient actions in that case would not be intelligent. This book does not intend to promote actions that compromise your integrity or blindly violate laws and regulations.

- Intelligent disobedience is *not* a form of protest against formal structures. Intelligently disobedient acts are performed only when required and only with a very specific beneficial intended outcome for the organization.
- Intelligent disobedience is *not* passive aggressive behavior. Indirectly resisting what others ask you to do is not intelligent disobedience; rather, intelligent disobedience represents the most fruitful, open, and intentional activity possible for the good of your organization. You communicate your intentions to your team, managers, and other stakeholders – *before* engaging in the act of intelligent disobedience, and ideally when your action is being considered and planned in advance. If you can't plan ahead of time, such as during a direct customer interaction when you need to respond immediately, communication to appropriate managers should take place as soon as possible after you have taken action.

You might ask, "Do I compromise my integrity if I engage in intelligent disobedience when I know my manager would not approve of my action?" Managers and their direct reports often have different perspectives on compliance versus possible results in specific situations. However, you do compromise your integrity if you proceed with intelligent disobedience when you have been specifically directed to refrain from a certain action, even when the benefits are evident. To determine whether proceeding despite your manager's direction is a valid act of intelligent disobedience, you must apply significant judgment to the circumstances. For your disobedience to be intelligent, you must justify how this interaction is different.

However, being told to refrain from acts of intelligent disobedience isn't the end of the story. Someone espousing intelligent disobedience would persistently seek to persuade their manager to reconsider their "under any circumstances" position. Instead of taking "no" as the final answer, you can try to apply intelligent disobedience in situations with less-than-optimal outcomes, seek to create small variances to existing processes, or promote a set of controlled parameters defining situations in which intelligent disobedience would be acceptable. The greater the potential outcomes are, the more persistent you should be in trying to obtain permission to engage in intelligent disobedience.

Note: This book does not provide guidelines for the appropriate magnitude of outcomes for engaging in intelligent disobedience, because individual circumstances can vary greatly. Nor does it specify a set of parameters around individual morality, because national, religious, and corporate norms and customs vary greatly around the world. You must assess these factors for yourself.

Doing your homework

Intelligent disobedience is powerful and risky. Done well, it can lead to positive outcomes for your business and your career. Done poorly, your actions can backfire and lead to considerable personal embarrassment. Before attempting intelligent disobedience, you must fully understand the environment you work in.

> ❝ *Before attempting intelligent disobedience, you must fully understand the environment you work in.* ❞

Understanding management's views is important in determining limitations and boundaries around acting with intelligent disobedience. In addition, you should consider more than just the procedural views of your manager when weighing the possibilities and consequences of an intelligently disobedient act. Following are additional items to evaluate to ensure that you are acting intelligently when varying from processes and organizational norms.

First, thoroughly understand any government regulations applicable to your company, position, industry, and relationship to the marketplace. I have yet to hear a story of intelligent disobedience in which breaking the law or violating regulatory requirements represented a constructive act of intelligent disobedience. I won't make an absolute statement that acts of intelligent disobedience *never* involve breaking government regulations, but these instances are rare. Use extreme caution when considering actions of intelligent disobedience involving regulatory compliance.

Second, corporate requirements and regulations also need to be fully understood. Many organizations have documents such as "Standards for employee behavior," "Business conduct guidelines," or "Standards for the management and treatment of vendors." Following guidelines is especially important when conducting a competitive bid process, because significant financial implications are at stake, and numerous entities can be affected positively or negatively by the outcome. Working within the processes outlined in documents of this nature can be just as important as maintaining integrity with government regulations.

The organization's corporate culture is another important factor. Culture is often a matter of pervasive behavioral expectations rather than a documented series of rules. Individuals joining an organization often hear about a subset of these norms. Many people attending my workshops who have attempted intelligent disobedience tell me that these expectations are mostly learned on the job.

These same individuals also state that corporate culture can be very straightforward, or very subtle and complex. Local and regional norms, international cultural expectations, and the expectations of major clients all have a bearing on how corporate culture manifests itself. How you work with your peers and colleagues and how you communicate with management are all subject to cultural norms. Whether you work directly with clients or are expected to work through marketing or account management teams, be sure to understand cultural expectations. Meeting etiquette and the use of email versus phone calls or face-to-face communication are also products of a company's culture. Take care to understand the cultural norms for areas that may be affected by your act of intelligent disobedience. If you aren't sure of a cultural expectation, ask your colleagues – especially those with history in the organization.

Successfully executing acts of intelligent disobedience requires that you understand your management team's parameters of success and failure in the eyes of their own superiors, the board, or primary stakeholders. For example, suppose that your management team is told they have brilliant marketing ideas, but those ideas cost too much to be sustainable. Your ability to execute intelligent disobedience is constrained by their focus on cost. They may like actions that save money, while disapproving of actions that yield more positive marketing outcomes, but cost more. Keep in mind that success and failure parameters can change over time, so you should ensure that you have up-to-date perspectives from your management team. Those parameters frequently change when a new senior manager is introduced.

Don't forget corporate strategy when considering acts of intelligent disobedience. While not all actions have a bearing on the implementation of strategy, I have been involved in acts of intelligent disobedience that promoted and acts that potentially detracted from stated corporate strategy. For example, I introduced a new product direction to an eager client before it was officially released as an offering – an action that was "against the rules." This act helped to promote a strategic direction, because the new offering was part of a shift in the organization's market position. The strategic direction touted by the management team was reinforced and promoted by having a client who viewed this new offering and received it favorably.

Conversely, I have occasionally acted with intelligent disobedience by doing things "the old way," which could have been interpreted as not supporting a new strategic direction. In one specific instance, a client needed support very quickly, and older processes were going to serve that client more favorably. This act, as with most appropriate acts of intelligent disobedience, was followed by considerable communication to explain the rationale for the action, as a means of calming fears about the acceptance of new strategies. Without understanding the strategic direction and the status of my organization in pursuing that strategy, my falling back on an older, familiar support process may have been viewed as "management disharmony." I may have been perceived as not supporting the company's strategic direction, and my actions would have diminished, if not eliminated, the perceived benefits to my attempt at intelligent disobedience.

Conclusion

The focus of intelligent disobedience is to achieve improved outcomes and about valuing improved performance over compliance with rules and customs, when appropriate. Intelligent disobedience is executed at any level of an organization, from employees on the coal face to senior executives. The most successful managers engage in intelligent disobedience and empower their staff to do the same.

Risk is a major consideration. Intelligent disobedience involves balancing personal and professional risks, assessing the business impacts of acting now versus later, achieving outcomes versus your personal image, and weighing the impact of noncompliance with rules and norms against improved outcomes.

Successfully engaging in intelligent disobedience requires understanding the short- and long-term implications of your actions or inaction. Considerable homework is required, including understanding management's viewpoints, government regulations, corporate culture and strategy.

Notes

1 "Steve" is not his real name. I will not be using real names in any of the stories conveyed in this book. I am using different names and company profiles to keep anonymous the managers and companies who put people in the position of committing acts of intelligent disobedience to achieve positive outcomes.
2 Chaleff, Ira. 2009. *The Courageous Follower: Standing up to and for Our Leaders.* 3rd ed. San Francisco, CA: Barrett-Koehler.

Chapter 2

Vanquishing remorse

In an article entitled "Why guts matter,"[1] US Senator John McCain states that the negative impacts of acting courageously will likely outweigh the realization that you were not authentic to your true self. You will probably regret not acting courageously.

> ❝ *the negative impacts of acting courageously will likely outweigh the realization that you were not authentic to your true self.* ❞

Regret is a temporary emotion that arises from situations that occur throughout our lives, whether it's wishing you hadn't eaten that fifth piece of pizza or regretting your decision to fight traffic over a holiday weekend. Remorse, on the other hand, is weighty and burdensome – something carried like excess baggage for a very long time. It is an emotion of emptiness stemming from missed opportunities or from sitting by passively when the right thing to do was to act.

Not acting with intelligent disobedience can lead to remorse. Once you appreciate the significance and longevity of remorse, that understanding can encourage you to embrace intelligent disobedience. Even if the results of an act of intelligent disobedience aren't what you'd hoped, the fact that you took action leaves you in a more positive emotional state.

This chapter describes a few true examples of instances in which missed opportunities and inaction caused remorse. If it seems a bit bleak, don't be put off. Keep reading! This chapter also identifies actions (or inactions) that produce remorse, to help you to recognize the early warning signs. You'll also find out how to fight negative emotions to find the courage to act with intelligent disobedience and to avoid remorse.

A lifetime of remorse

My father was a man of few words. Even rarer were words he spoke about himself. He was the sort of a man you would expect to have grown from a Depression-era baby, the son of Irish immigrants in Connecticut, USA. He worked hard, strived to follow directions, worked for large organizations, and retired in his mid-60s. He was an advocate for what he felt was right, but ultimately he entrusted his work life to his superiors.

On his deathbed, my father confided a deeply held, private belief about his life.

"Please don't repeat my mistake. I was never aggressive enough in pursuit of myself."

My father was not expressing regret. This sharing was about remorse – an emptiness that followed my father to his grave.

I, too, have experienced remorse, not only from watching my dad, but from my own experience. The reason I am so passionate about intelligent disobedience is because I have no intention of adding excess baggage to my professional or personal life. However, I wasn't always smart or courageous enough to avoid remorse by practicing intelligent disobedience.

Early in my management career, my own manager asked me to take responsibility for driving a strategic initiative. Our part of the business needed to be involved in this initiative, but the organization chart called for a different department to lead the initiative. What my manager asked me to do was contrary to the defined accountabilities for our business areas. Initially – and only briefly – I challenged my manager about his request, concerned that I should not be the one leading the initiative. He told me it was what he wanted and that he would back me up in any conflict over responsibilities. I left his office with my marching orders and proceeded to try to lead the initiative.

The result was a disaster. To this day, this situation epitomizes to me the "cost of silence." Although my manager tried to support me, the diversion from agreed-upon responsibilities was not well received. We struggled. We spent money, and we squandered time and talent. But we could not overcome the erosion of trust brought about by trying to lead from the wrong area of the business. The initiative failed. Some senior managers in the organization viewed me negatively. Most impactful, I lost friends and the trust of competent, professional colleagues. I will always carry that remorse with me.

What causes remorse?

In intelligent disobedience workshops, most attendees identify several actions or inactions that generate remorse in the workplace:

- taking a course of action you believe is unproductive or detrimental;
- standing on the sidelines and watching something fall short of expectations;
- failing to follow through on a strong, intuitive thought; and/or
- supporting or taking an action that compromises your integrity.

Remorse develops over time

Remorse resulting from the wrong decision doesn't present immediately; it usually progresses through stages of increasingly intense emotions. In my earlier example of leadership responsibility, I started out a bit *apprehensive*; the assignment I was given did not seem right and I questioned it. As the initiative proceeded and progress became more difficult, I began to *fear* that I was not going to succeed. As the negative outcomes became apparent, I tried to reverse them, but I wasn't addressing the core issue of where leadership should have been based. I felt a sense of *emptiness* as I watched things slip away. Finally, since the end of the failed initiative, I have experienced *remorse*, which stays with me.

The emotional path from apprehension, through fear and emptiness, to remorse is a story I've heard frequently. Sometimes, people progress quickly through each emotion; sometimes, it takes many months. However, each story ends the same way: with an emotional burden that isn't easily discarded.

The good news is that you can use this progression to your advantage. Once you recognize that you're on a path of increasingly negative emotions, you can employ intelligent disobedience to prevent them from going further. In addition, your understanding of the negative emotions and outcomes can help you to overcome any hesitation or fear of acting with intelligent disobedience.

Positive intent is the antidote to remorse

People rarely express remorse over actions they undertook with positive intent, even if those actions failed. Falling short of achieving the right outcome might create regrets, but those are temporary and something we can quickly learn from. People consistently express satisfaction with "trying to do what was right."

This point is reinforced whenever we ask people to share the last time they did *not* follow their intuition, leading to detrimental results. The stories flow quickly during this exercise; the negative emotions are still strong regardless of how long ago the situation occurred. In contrast, when asked to share the last time they followed their intuition with a negative outcome, very few stories emerge – and when they do, the instances of regret or remorse are rare. Acting and failing has much less impact, over the long term, than failing to act and dealing with the results.

Trusting your intuition

Suppose you don't have facts indicating the likelihood of negative outcomes, and all you have is an *intuition* that bad things will happen. If you ignore your intuition, you still risk long-term emotional consequences. It's okay – even necessary – to act based on intuition when you don't have all the facts.

Intuition may be challenging as justification for action in the workplace. In most organizations, nonstandard actions require additional support from management (either before or after the action is taken). Most managers want to analyze facts, especially when considering something that strays from defined corporate processes. So approaching management with a hunch and asking for support might seem like a doomed endeavor.

As it turns out, surveys demonstrate that people underestimate the value that managers place on intuition. My company conducted a poll in which we asked managers to imagine they were hiring a new project manager. They were asked to decide between two candidates who were equal in every way, but one. The difference? One candidate was an expert in process management, while the other had superior intuition. Of the 260+ managers who responded to the survey, 93 percent said that they would select the intuitive candidate.

Based on the results of that survey, we now recommend to our clients that they share intuition with management. The key is to be honest that you are using your intuition. Some managers, who may have that same intuition, may approve the proposed response. If a manager doesn't agree, we recommend that you propose actions you can take to validate your intuition and, once it is validated, engage in an intelligently disobedient act. This approach has been very effective. It's also helped my teams to avoid the apprehension that comes from supporting intuitive approaches. And, more importantly, it's helped to avoid undesired outcomes and remorse.

The problem with avoiding discomfort

Not taking action is typically a short-term decision to avoid discomfort, but one that germinates a seed of more deep-rooted discomfort. According to many of our workshop attendees, what blocks them from engaging in acts of intelligent disobedience is the desire to avoid the difficult conversation required or to bypass the scrutiny that comes with intelligent disobedience. Even when people understand the risk and significance of feeling remorse, hesitation comes from a certainty that some degree of discomfort will result. This "certain discomfort" overshadows the highly likely, yet future, discomfort of watching from the sidelines as something goes awry.

The avoidance of discomfort triggers a memory for me. When I was young, I loved watching demolition derbies. Contestants drive older cars and collide with each other on purpose, the objective being to disable other vehicles, while not rendering your own car inoperable. The driver whose car is the last one running is the winner.

If you try to avoid hitting other vehicles in a demolition derby, you will be disqualified. If you sit in your car and don't move, other drivers will eventually hit your car to ensure that it stops running. The bottom line: you snooze, you lose. You might avoid the risk of damaging your car, but you'll lose the contest.

People are following this same losing strategy when they avoid short-term discomfort when an act of intelligent disobedience is clearly necessary. Wanting to be part of substantive change in your business is like a demolition derby: to win, you must endure a bump or two.

But why would you want to subject yourself to bumps and bruises to make something positive happen? To answer this question, let's go back to my father's comment about not "aggressively pursuing himself."

You may be in a job you love, which doesn't require you to stretch your skills. You may not have to take the risks associated with intelligent disobedience – and that's fine. If you don't have a compelling reason to engage in intelligent disobedience, you shouldn't. However, I recommend that you be honest with yourself as you reflect on whether you are apprehensive about:

- what's going on with your work;
- how your career is progressing;
- the business outcomes you and your group produce; and
- the content of the deliverables or services you are providing.

If you aren't apprehensive, great! In that case, this section of the book is for potential future reference. But if you are apprehensive or wish for something more, you risk placing yourself on the long-term emotional freefall from apprehension to remorse. You probably aren't "pursuing yourself."

My father's obedience, sticking to a career path laid out and controlled by his managers, left him feeling empty. He took advice that was conservative and not always given with his best interests in mind. He didn't take many risks until very late in his career – and, even then, he took those risks as an advocate for others rather than for himself. (He was an auditor for a regulatory body providing governance oversight of public utility companies.) My father didn't argue with his boss easily and would shrug off unfounded complaints by others if the only way of resolving them involved emotional confrontation. He was an intelligent man, and he worked hard to research and lay out *facts* that would speak for themselves before taking any action. But if people did not listen to facts and posed *emotional* arguments instead, he rarely pushed back. That's one of the things my Dad meant when he said he was not pursuing himself: he didn't always defend his point of view.

That's what I think happens when you settle for the status quo or follow instructions that you believe will yield suboptimal outcomes: you simply aren't expressing the best of who you are, which can launch you on the pathway towards remorse.

How to outwit fear

This section describes several techniques you can use to overcome your fears, so that you can engage in intelligent disobedience.

Look past immediate discomfort and focus on what's right

Someone who worked hard to avoid remorse was Roger Boisjoly, who worked for Morton Thiokol as an engineer. He led a team tasked with improving performance of the O-rings for the solid rocket boosters for NASA's Space Shuttle.[2] The failure of those O-rings caused the explosion of the shuttle Challenger in January 1986, 73 seconds after launch. The explosion killed all seven astronauts, including Christa McAuliffe, a civilian who was to be the first teacher in space.

The forecast for the launch day of Challenger was unusually cold weather. A team of NASA managers, engineers, and technical team members met the evening before the scheduled launch to discuss the possibilities and concerns for launching in those conditions. There was genuine concern, because a shuttle had never been launched in anywhere near the forecast 31°F (−1°C) temperature, following a predicted overnight low temperature of 18°F (−7.8°C). The representatives at the meeting were supposed to share their opinions on the risks of launching. The lives of the astronauts and the reputations of the companies who partnered to drive the Space Shuttle program were at stake. In addition, US President Ronald Reagan was planning to reference the Challenger mission during his annual State of the Union Address the day after the launch, which added political pressure to the decision to remain on schedule.

As a representative in this meeting, Boisjoly faced a decision. If he were honest and expressed concerns, he would admit that the O-ring performance might be affected at cold temperatures. That was the conservative position to take, although there was no specific data on the performance of the rings at the forecast temperature. Boisjoly had, however, been trying to emphasize the significant weaknesses in the O-rings to his superiors at Morton Thiokol and NASA for much of the year prior to the Challenger launch. Expressing those concerns in this launch decision forum would raise doubt that his company's product could perform within NASA's contracted performance parameters. Despite pressure placed upon him by his management team, he expressed his concern and recommended against a launch. After some deliberation and despite his concerns, a decision was made and the shuttle was launched the next morning. Shortly after launch, one of the O-rings on a solid rocket booster failed, and a flare of burning gas escaped from the solid booster, causing a fuel tank to explode, destroying the shuttle and all aboard.

Boisjoly had engaged in intelligent disobedience, contrary to the directions from his management team. His action was uncomfortable – and even more so after the accident. However, Boisjoly knew that he took the correct position. He reported enduring ongoing discomfort from his company and peers.[3] He eventually left the company, and he switched his focus to lecturing on engineering ethics across the world. He received significant backlash from his corporate leaders, but had the benefit of knowing that he had proposed action that could have avoided a disaster. In recognition of his ethical position and fortitude, he received the Prize for Scientific Freedom and Responsibility from the American Association for the Advancement of Science.

Thankfully, not all decisions about engaging intelligent disobedience involve life or death situations. However, most options involving intelligent disobedience do involve some risk, in addition to dealing with potential remorse.

Provide information to foster understanding instead of confronting

A former colleague of mine demonstrated how to reduce both personal risk and the potential for experiencing remorse when challenging superiors. His name is Stephan, and he pulled off a fabulous act of intelligent disobedience.

Stephan worked as a manager for the military. He was directing one project as part of a larger program of work. The program was delivering value, but was not the highest priority in the group's agenda. His program team had started to receive emails from their senior officers at the Pentagon questioning the content of the program. The emails indicated an incomplete understanding of all aspects of the program. As a result, Stephan and the team grew concerned that the program would be cancelled. After a couple of months, their suspicions were confirmed: they received word their program was being cancelled to fund other initiatives.

The members of the program team felt betrayal and grief. Stephan felt those emotions, too, but he also sensed something else: that an inappropriate decision-making process was in place. The program had been cancelled based on partially accurate information, as reflected in the emails that his team had received and the questions that had been asked. Stephan decided that was not what his superiors would have wanted, and – despite the risks involved with questioning senior officers at the Pentagon – he decided to act. Stephan emailed a reply to his superiors at the Pentagon.

In the email, he recognized the decision to cancel the program and also conveyed his concern that the decision was made with incomplete information. While expressing an understanding that priorities can change and his support for those changes, he shared his thoughts on the potential misconceptions about the program. He laid out the questions he believed needed to be asked to appropriately weigh the program's value against that of other programs in the group's portfolio. He also provided answers to those questions. In conclusion, he stated that his objective was to ensure that decisions were being made with the most complete and accurate information, because that is what he would want if he were in a position of authority.

The day after he had sent this email, Stephan received a call, directing him to fly to the Pentagon to attend a meeting to discuss the program. At the meeting, people well above Stephan's rank asked him for more details about the program and his views on how it was being managed. They also explored various aspects of the benefits that could be achieved by the program. When the meeting concluded, the program funding was restored, and Stephan was promoted to program manager to implement the program and achieve its potential benefits.

The notable points about this story are as follows.

- Stephan did not explicitly ask for anything in his email; rather, he offered additional information in appreciation of the challenges inherent in the busy roles of his superiors.
- He expressed an understanding and support of the decisions that had to be made.
- While it could be characterized as pushback or an escalation that challenged the Pentagon's decision, Stephan' primary focus was on providing additional information. Directly and openly challenging a decision in the US military would have been unlikely to be received in such a positive manner.

While not all situations calling for an act of intelligent disobedience can be addressed in the manner Stephan deployed, seeking to add richness to a conversation is usually a very effective technique. His passion for ensuring that the best information was available avoided the feeling of remorse and, in Stephan's mind, might have helped others to avoid feeling remorse as well.

"If I were in a position of authority and I had made the decision to cancel that program from the information being provided initially, I suspect I would have felt remorse if I discovered the more complete story later on," said Stephan.

Interestingly, Stephan's actions spoke clearly, saying "this is not a good decision" without ever directly questioning that decision at all! We revisit this story and discuss other intelligently disobedient techniques throughout this book.

Focus on positive outcomes that would be missed

Stephan's story also brings up another form of remorse avoidance: envisioning positive outcomes that would be missed if intelligent disobedience were not undertaken. In other words, you need to recognize that a positive outcome won't come to fruition without some action as a catalyst.

Use "buckets" to identify what you can change

Unfortunately, even with intelligent disobedience, we aren't always able to bring outcomes to fruition because we don't have the necessary authority. Does that mean that remorse is inevitable or that it's acceptable to do nothing? Not at all. But it might require framing the problem differently. This is where the "bucket approach" can help. Instead of thinking, "I cannot change this; it's tied to corporate culture, and I cannot change the culture," think about where you *can* act. Break your thinking into "A bucket", "B-bucket," and "C-bucket" activities.

Here's how it works.

A-bucket activities are actions that you can take within your own team or department with only a minimal need for permission to proceed. Even though you might not be able to change your organization's culture or overall procedures, you might be able to work with your teammates and convince them that a change in approach would be beneficial. If you then engage in that new approach and get positive results, you're on your way! You then take these positive results to engage in B-bucket activities.

B-bucket activities are actions you can take by demonstrating prior success and trying to influence others in your direct network of relationships to do the same. Within your company, your direct network could include other managers and peers who know and respect you. For users of the LinkedIn business network application, direct network connections would be first-level contacts whom you might or might not talk with on a regular basis. Sharing the changes or improvements you made and the success that resulted could influence them to try those changes as well. If they succeed, then your change is spreading and, at some point, could go viral. You can further try to spread your change by asking your direct networks to share their success with others (essentially, the second-level contacts in a LinkedIn network). Even if you get unfavorable feedback from this network of connections, you can use that feedback to refine your approach, if appropriate.

After you receive and process feedback, you can proceed to **C-bucket** activities, where your change and success story is laid out for senior managers in the hope that refined policies and procedures will result.

With crafty networking or a bit of luck, you can sometimes jump from A-bucket to C-bucket changes if your network has the appropriate contacts. Such a jump occurred during a consulting engagement that I managed at a major US financial services company.

While my team was providing services to our client, we were subject to the client's "rules of engagement" for working with contractors. After working successfully for several months, those engagement rules changed, which required the deployment of awkward processes for our engagement. Overall, the change was positive for our client. However, some of the changes wasted time and money for my team and the client, because of the circumstances of our particular outsourced services arrangement. Via an appeals process, we proposed changes to the new rules of engagement to suit our contracted arrangement, but the change recommendations were rejected.

We started some A-bucket activities, which sought to satisfy the new rules, while also varying the approach taken to track my team's activities. We were gaining some support for our approaches when a client steering committee member was invited to a roundtable discussion with his CEO. We asked if he could bring up the restrictions that the new rules of engagement were imposing on our contractual arrangement. We outlined how those restrictions would create difficulties for other services-outsourcing arrangements. Our steering committee member agreed and successfully discussed the situation with his CEO, who gained an understanding of the situation and shared his thoughts with his management team. Soon thereafter, we successfully worked with the client team to negotiate changes to the new rules of engagement for contractors.

Are you powerless?

To avoid remorse, the key is to realize that there are few situations in which you are powerless. The bucket approach can help – especially if you're working in an organization that has resisted change or in which staff members have acquired a sense of learned helplessness.

"Learned helplessness" is a term and condition defined by American psychologist Martin E.P. Seligman. Per the *Encyclopedia Britannica*, "Seligman coined the term learned helplessness to describe the expectation that outcomes are uncontrollable."[4]

Learned helplessness has since become a basic principle of behavioral theory, demonstrating that prior learning can result in a drastic change in behavior, and seeking to explain why individuals may accept and remain passive in negative situations despite their clear ability to change them.

Intelligent disobedience workshop attendees report having encountered behaviors that reflect this condition. When changes are too big for their span of control, many people retreat from any active pursuit of a change in the business environment, cultural expectations, or process changes. Learned helplessness bogs down any pursuit of improvement for those who wish to stimulate improvements in the workplace.

Learned helplessness is a recipe for remorse. Using the bucket approach to frame your thinking and "a sales pitch for change" with your peers and subordinates helps you to avoid learned helplessness behaviors.

Conclusion

Deciding to mitigate the risk of experiencing remorse and to engage in an act of intelligent disobedience is a personal journey. That journey is different for everyone, based on personal history and risk aversion. The consequences of this journey, however, involve outcomes that last much longer than a night's drive home or a relaxed weekend to shed the pressures of the prior work week.

This chapter is meant to help you to reflect on the long-term implications of actions taken or not taken when faced with positive or negative outcomes in business. I do not wish to pass judgment or prescribe a set of specific rules for deciding whether to engage in an act of intelligent disobedience. The decision is yours, based on your thoughts, intuitions, values, personal goals, and ambitions.

By examining your own risk profile relative to actions you could take, you can improve outcomes or avoid setbacks. As a trusted colleague says, "Control your own destiny or someone else will!" What's more, reflecting on the quote from my father at the beginning of this chapter, I want to help you to "pursue yourself" more completely as you seek to generate more positive outcomes in your work life.

Notes

1 McCain, John, 2004. Why guts matter. *Fast Company*, September, 56.
2 Online Ethics Center (OEC). 2016. Roger Boisjoly: the Challenger disaster [Online]. Available at: http://www.onlineethics.org/cms/7123.aspx [Accessed 24 January 2017].
3 National Public Radio, Inc. (NPR). 2012. Remembering Roger Boisjoly: he tried to stop shuttle Challenger launch [Online]. Available at: http://www.npr.org/sections/thetwo-way/2012/02/06/146490064/remembering-roger-boisjoly-he-tried-to-stop-shuttle-challenger-launch [Accessed 24 January 2017].
4 Nolen, Jeannette, L. 2009. Learned helplessness. *Encyclopaedia Britannica* [Online] Available at: https://www.britannica.com/topic/learned-helplessness [Accessed 1 February 2017].

Chapter 3

A higher form of ethics

Considering the ethics of acts of intelligent disobedience is beneficial, because intelligent disobedience involves acting counter to management directions or bypassing widely held business processes. However, appropriate acts of intelligent disobedience frequently reflect a *higher* form of ethics, because you engage in acts that support the greater good of your organization. In this chapter, we will evaluate intelligent disobedience from an ethical standpoint, using the behavioral boundaries and conditions described in previous chapters. The chapter also examines how these actions might represent a higher degree of ethical behavior. While general and widely applicable guidelines will be discussed, it should be noted that situations differ, which may alter the considerations presented in this chapter.

The fundamentals of ethical intelligent disobedience

Engaging in ethical intelligent disobedience requires firm adherence to the behavioral boundaries discussed in the first chapter. As a review, acting with intelligent disobedience means that you

- do *not* perform acts that benefit yourself rather than the business;
- do *not* violate process or take other unusual actions as a matter of course (remembering that acts of intelligent disobedience are performed to achieve a specific outcome for the business when standard practices do not yield the desired outcome);
- do *not* engage in nonstandard activities as a form of protest against formal structures or processes;
- do *not* engage in passive aggressive behavior (remembering that indirectly resisting what others ask you to do is not intelligent disobedience).

Respect for the individual: sharing the truth

My views on ethics were formed early in my career when I kept hearing the phrase "respect for the individual" again and again. That phrase refers not only to addressing people mindfully and truthfully in one-on-one interactions, but also to evaluating every interaction to ensure that you communicate with clarity and transparency. In addition, information exchanged in interactions should reflect the truth as you understand it. That truth should accurately depict news – whether it's good, bad, or a little bit of both. If the scenarios you share paint a complete and accurate picture for the people with whom you interact, you are conducting yourself in an ethical manner.

When considering breaking or bending closely held and treasured processes, questions regarding the ethical way of proceeding should be front of mind. However, the framework for ethical behavior in the context of intelligent disobedience isn't always clear-cut.

The following are some questions to help you to evaluate the ethics of an act of intelligent disobedience.

- Will any information you convey potentially deceive others?
- Are you considering withholding information from others?
- Will your action benefit your area of the business, while potentially negatively impacting another?

If the answer to any of these questions is "yes" – or even "maybe" – then you should re-evaluate whether you are considering an ethical act of intelligent disobedience.

Unethical approaches: the risks of acting impulsively and not acting at all

The most significant ethical issues discussed in intelligent disobedience workshops arise from lack of action or acting without appropriate forethought. For example, if you see or believe that your business is engaging in activities that aren't beneficial and you don't share your concerns, you are not behaving ethically. The same is true if you have evidence that a course of action will not benefit the business, yet you do nothing. Stories from notable individuals and the following definition of ethics back up this premise:

> *Behaving ethically requires action in both positive and negative circumstances.*

Behaving ethically requires action in both positive and negative circumstances.

Acting ethically may seem like it should be simple. However, it isn't that easy. Concerns about "rocking the boat," and trying to balance personal and business relationships, and pressures to meet ever-rising business expectations make us act impulsively or freeze when action is prudent.

The tendency to act impulsively and the dangers of doing so are the topic of a *Harvard Business Review* article[1] that discusses how difficult it can be to act ethically "in the moment" in day-to-day business situations. When presented with ethical decisions in workshops, people consistently choose appropriately; yet those same people are not as likely to make the right choices in the day-to-day world of work. This discrepancy is the result of the pressure to perform and the very short time frames that people have in which to think things through.

Even very successful people at the top of an organization sometimes don't act or speak up when they should. Warren Buffett has said, "Too often I was silent when management made proposals that I judged to be counter to the interests of shareholders . . . collegiality

> " *Too often I was silent when management made proposals that I judged to be counter to the interests of shareholders . . . collegiality trumped independence.* "

trumped independence."[2] The desire to belong can tempt you to lose authenticity in your beliefs and "the truth" that has crafted your unique life experiences and beliefs. This dilemma can be a desperate struggle, even for the strong-willed. Ensuring that acts of intelligent disobedience are prudent and ethical requires taking the time to think through options clearly and, when possible, sharing your idea with a trusted colleague before acting.

A silent ethical group could be on your side, supporting your ethical intelligent disobedience

Well-thought-out acts of intelligent disobedience can uncover support groups you did not even know existed. Ethical acts of intelligent disobedience often receive significant support from a broad set of individuals. Their opinions may be revealed only when someone engaging in intelligent disobedience has the courage to speak up or to take a difficult action.

I once had the sad experience of having to fire an engaging, popular member of a team for lack of performance. His social skills provided benefit to the team and stakeholders, but these were overshadowed by a lack of accuracy and completeness in his business deliverables. I struggled with the decision to dismiss him, because duty to the business and the team's technical output were pitted against risks to the team's cohesiveness and potential backlash against his dismissal. However, dismissal was the appropriate action despite the risks.

We announced his departure and prepared for a difficult aftermath. That aftermath never emerged. In fact, the opposite occurred. Most team members expressed sadness at their colleague's departure, while also expressing relief and gratitude, because he had been making things more difficult. As was the case for Warren Buffett, collegiality had suppressed complaints about their well-liked colleague and had hidden a pervasive desire for change.

Is intelligent disobedience "playing politics"?

Our workshop attendees often question the ethical nature of intelligent disobedience, viewing it as a disguised form of manipulating others or playing politics. As mentioned earlier, if you act with the intent of achieving personal gain, then the question of ethics is a valid one. If your objective is to teach others or improve your organization's effectiveness, then you're on sound ethical standing, and you are not playing politics at all. Each situation is different, however, so we will discuss ethics using several examples.

Let's examine the situation and actions surrounding the polarizing story of Edward Snowden.[3] Snowden was launched into the news spotlight when he revealed the activities of the US National Security Administration (NSA) through confidential information that he provided to journalists.

I do not have enough information to draw appropriate conclusions about whether his was an appropriate act of intelligent disobedience – but the following are some questions that can help us to clarify the validity and ethics of Snowden's actions, if the questions could be answered completely.

- Was Snowden prompted to act by a desire for self-promotion or did he firmly believe that the NSA was acting beyond its fiduciary and ethical boundaries?
- Prior to taking action, were objections raised with the management team? Did Snowden, with positive intent and diligent fact-gathering, persistently raise his objections to his management team?
- Were negative, as well as positive, outcomes thoroughly evaluated? Did Snowden consider that legitimate and critical security structures could be rendered useless as a result of the release of data? If so, did he consider alternative ways of revealing information without endangering these structures?
- Was there evidence that the action supported the greater good and beliefs of the larger population? Did Snowden have evidence that he would be acting to support the interest and beliefs of the majority of Americans, or simply his

own personal view of what was right and wrong? (Intelligent disobedience supports taking action in alignment with your own personal views of ethical behavior. If Snowden was not certain he was acting in the best ethical interests of the majority of Americans, one alternative would have been to quit his job, separating himself from what he thought was inappropriate activity. He could then – without releasing confidential data – have attempted to share the type of activity that was occurring. We can only speculate on what might have been the results of that approach.)

History may reveal the answers to these questions, resulting in rich conversations about the applicability of intelligent disobedience in this instance. In the meantime, these questions provide context and consideration for forming our own thoughts on the ethics of intelligent disobedience, particularly when our action might affect others who can't participate in the decision to act with intelligent disobedience.

A second example of ethics versus playing politics (literally) was unfolding at the time I was writing this book. Sally Yates, Acting US Attorney General, was fired by newly inaugurated US President Donald Trump. Yates, upon reading an executive order issued by President Trump that placed travel restrictions on citizens of seven predominantly Muslim countries, refused to defend the order, declaring it unconstitutional. The order stipulated that travel privileges for citizens of those countries would be withdrawn until more extensive immigration evaluation processes could be put in place.[4] Newspapers reported confusion at the nation's border ports, as well as protests across the nation, including within the university and corporate sectors. Yates, on the basis of her belief that the order was unconstitutional, instructed her department to refrain from enforcing the order. In public defiance of the president, she expressed her ethical and legal stance on the matter, and promptly lost her job. These actions could be evaluated using the same types of question posed in relation to Snowden's actions, to determine the appropriateness of Yates' act of intelligent disobedience.

A similar, but less weighty, ethical decision arises when deciding to take action to manage office politics. Authenticity is the recommended ethical criterion when considering political action in an office setting. In a personal example, an employee of mine tried to engage in intelligent disobedience by means of bypassing some organizational hierarchies. A lack of authenticity made that disobedience something less than intelligent.

I had taken on a management role in a new organization. Within a few days, I had an enthusiastic, confident, and capable employee scheduling time on my calendar to share ideas. I encouraged this, because I believed his thoughts had merit.

As discussions continued, he extended social invitations, since my new management role involved relocating. I accepted some of his invitations, with limits to avoid favoritism. My employee expressed appreciation for sharing this time together. A couple of months later, I had to make a business decision that affected this employee. I listened to and considered his views, but decided against the alternative he believed was best. After announcing my decision, the employee did not speak to me again professionally or socially; and often went out of his way to avoid doing so, even when I tried to initiate conversations.

I drew the following conclusions from this scenario.

- His actions appeared to have been an attempt to manipulate me for personal gain.
- His lack of follow-up on the decision, or any subsequent business scenario, changed my perception of his capabilities and confidence.
- His actions and statements were likely not authentic, which compromised my trust in him. This erosion of trust was compounded by his lack of contact after I made the decision that disappointed him.

Many business scenarios call for managing relationships with key decision makers or influencers with whom you might not otherwise develop a relationship. Based on your organization's culture, relationships may or may not involve social, as well as business, interactions. Judgment is critical here as to the appropriateness and extent to which you develop and nurture these relationships. Authenticity and ethics go hand in hand in these situations. Although authenticity is a mostly subjective measure, it is helpful to ask yourself, "Would I say or do this if I did not have a business objective to achieve?" If the answer is "no," reconsidering your actions is called for. One approach is to take action: to attend those events (both business and social) that your business calls for, but limit what you say in those settings, so that you don't compromise your authenticity and damage trust.

Educating and informing versus deceiving

A significant act of intelligent disobedience is to let an activity fail to deliver promised outcomes. Suppose enthusiastic, but inexperienced, individuals want to pursue an ill-conceived course of action, despite your recommendation of other alternatives. Allowing your colleagues to pursue their chosen course of action can be an effective way of educating them. Although potentially detrimental to the business in the short term, the experience and lessons learned by dedicated team members can yield benefits for years to come. Appropriately managing this intelligently disobedient technique is a good example of the ethics being espoused in this chapter.

To ethically manage allowing something to fail, you must ensure the following.

- There must be absolutely no spite involved. This technique should not involve a silent competition between you and a colleague; it is performed for educational purposes only. (*You* will learn something if the approach surprises you and works; *others* learn if the failure you expect comes to fruition.)
- The extent of any failure must be small and contained, occur early, and be able to be recovered quickly and cheaply.
- You must not deceive management regarding the activity. Don't communicate confidence in the outcome when you believe the result will be failure. Instead, tout the learning achieved whether the pursued techniques work or the expected failure occurs. In addition, communicate how you plan to contain the extent of the failure to preserve the integrity of your business.

Note: Should your colleagues or team members often push approaches that are different rom those that you promote, an examination of why your experience and opinions aren't being valued is in order.

Carla, the account manager discussed in Chapter 1, demonstrated another version of informing versus deceiving. Carla was faced with a dilemma: should she follow the sales direction established by her marketing manager's sales approach, or should she act in what she believes to be the best interest of her client? Carla framed the dilemma as an ethics issue. To maintain her integrity with her marketing manager, she needed to follow his direction; simultaneously, she wanted to maintain her integrity with her client and propose pragmatic solutions. Doing both was the approach that Carla deemed ethical.

In a meeting with her client management team, Carla shared the new marketing and product approach that her company advocated, and then proposed an altered product mix to meet her client's needs. Her client was impressed with her transparency and adopted her product mix strategy. In addition, the client chose elements of the new product marketing direction that Carla's company was promoting to support a new initiative.

Appropriately acting beyond your scope of responsibility

Acting beyond your scope of responsibility is a form of intelligent disobedience – but you must consider the ethics of acting in this manner.

Consider this example.

Ian, a technology manager for an international oil and gas equipment company, is diligently working to ensure that his company has up-to-date technology, while managing tight budgetary restrictions. It's late in the calendar year, and he is the covering manager while many of his senior peers have started their holidays. A vendor calls, offering special discounts for volume purchases of a product that Ian's company needs. The offer from the vendor is favorable, but presents challenges for Ian.

- The per unit price offered is less than the company planned to pay, but the number of units required for the discount is more than it had planned to procure. The company could use the additional products, so procuring them at the proposed discount would be advantageous.
- The offer from the vendor expires on 31 December, and Ian does not have the delegated authority to make the purchase without permission from the senior management council, which will not meet until after the deadline.
- The procurement costs would exceed the company's spending plan for this calendar year, but would save a considerable sum in the overall technology upgrade planned for the following year. It is a good deal in the longer term.
- Making the purchase is in the long-term interest of the company, but executing a purchase contract of this size without senior management council approval would be a significant violation of the company's delegated authority rules.

On the one hand, Ian does not believe it is ethical to violate the delegated authority rules; on the other, he has a great offer in front of him. After some consideration, Ian tries to contact the members of the council. Because of the holidays, it is a bit of a struggle, but he has some success. He reaches three of the council members, all of whom agree that he should proceed with the purchase because of the long-term benefits to the company. He cannot reach the other Council members. The procurement rules specify that ratification of large purchases require a majority of the seven senior management council members to vote positively.

Ian decides that an act of intelligent disobedience is in order, and he signs the purchase contract. The rationale that he later conveys to the Council is that:

- he had no opportunity to wait until the council met again to take advantage of this pricing, and the overall cost was favorable;
- he had discussed the situation with as many of the council members as he could and had received a unanimously positive response;

- because he was covering for his manager, who was a member of the council, he would have strongly recommended making the purchase, and while he knew that his delegated authority did not give him a formal vote on council matters, he would have made his recommendation to the council at large;
- he felt without a doubt that signing the purchase contract was in the best interests of the company, and although he did violate the procurement rules, he followed those rules to the greatest degree he could, given the circumstances.

When the senior leaders return to work, the council discussed Ian's action. Concerns were raised, and the council tells Ian that he should not again act beyond the scope of his delegated authority. However, the council does recognize the unique circumstances of the situation and believes that Ian acted with the best interests of the overall business in mind. He is not formally praised during the council meeting, but receives informal praise from many of the council members.

Using power ethically

Former US President John Adams said, "Because power corrupts, society's demands for moral authority and character increase as the importance of the position increases."[5]

With a mandate to accomplish difficult things, leaders can and do leverage the power or authority they have within their organizations. Much of that power is formal – that is, it comes with the position or role. Formal authority provides a powerful platform from which to engage in intelligent disobedience. However, just about anyone in an organization can leverage other forms of power or authority – with good or not-so-good outcomes. Regardless of the position you hold, if you consider leveraging your power or authority to engage in intelligent disobedience, you should ensure that you act with moral authority and character, as the second US President John Adams stated.

Let's examine different forms of power and some common ethical issues that can arise. While many of the following issues can be driven by any type of authority, we will discuss the most common temptations initiated by different types of authority.

> **Positional authority** comes with a managerial position, as defined by a company's organization chart. This is the most formal and recognized type of authority, and typically includes the direct management of individuals, involving determination of pay, performance assessment, and nomination for promotion or transfer. This role is perfect for providing guidance and boundaries

for individuals to follow when considering acts of intelligent disobedience. It also represents an opportunity to instruct a subordinate to perform an act of intelligent disobedience. However, this power can be easily abused.

The following are guidelines to consider when assigning acts of intelligent disobedience to others.

- The manager who directs a subordinate to perform an act of intelligent diso- bedience is responsible for defending those actions, not the employee who performs them. If you use positional power to delegate intelligent disobedi- ence to others, you should pave the way for those actions in advance (when possible) and/or directly deal with any stakeholders who express concerns about the actions taken. Do not make your employee deal with the issues that may arise.
- You should be willing to explicitly document the act of intelligent disobe- dience that you directed another person to take. If you are unwilling or, if questioned, would hesitate to admit that direction, reconsider the intelligent disobedience action that you are pondering.

Referential authority arises when you refer to someone else as a means of expanding your personal power. For example, you have significant ref- erential authority when you report directly to the CEO and regularly take action on her behalf. If you say "Joan (the CEO) sent me to ask you to do something," you are likely to get the same response as if you were the CEO. Referential authority works, is valid, and should be used to drive actions and accomplishments. However, you are abusing this authority type in the following circumstances.

- You say that your boss said something when she didn't. Doing so is prob- ably not appropriate even if you believe that she would support your premise or she would say it if you were to ask her. You may be acting with what you believe are your boss's intentions, but attributing statements or directions to your boss that she did not say can get both of you in trouble. An act of intelligent disobedience that focuses on your actions or decisions may have an ethical standing. It exceeds ethical boundaries if your use of referential authority puts another person – like your boss – in an uncom- fortable position.
- You assume that you have referential power or authority over anything not explicitly given to you by your boss. Although you may be trying to act in her best interests, the potential for getting your boss in hot water means that your actions may not be ethical.

The best way of avoiding these ethical situations is to have explicit conversations with your boss, so that you understand the limitations to your referential authority and your boss's boundaries around allowing you to act with intelligent disobedience.

Expert authority comes from your depth of experience. For example, if you were the designer of your insurance company's last several medical insurance offerings, you would probably not need a formal management position to give you considerable power. People would recognize you as the expert and follow your recommendations. Put simply, you can influence others via the knowledge you have and the ideas you propose. Because this type of power can be very effective, the following are some guidelines to help you to avoid abusing it.

- Do *not* exaggerate the benefits or pitfalls of an action. You should not oversell the issues or opportunities that you see as a means of getting your way; instead, present your expert opinion, and let the facts speak for themselves. If you suspect something is good or bad, but don't have the facts, identify your statements as suspicions, not facts. Otherwise, you are abusing your power.
- Do *not* imply that your expertise is broader than it is. For instance, you may be deeply involved with your company's medical insurance offerings, but not the auto insurance products. While you may have opinions about auto insurance, you should not give the impression that your opinions about auto insurance come from the same level of expertise that you have with medical insurance.

Personal authority (also known as **power of personality**) is the power that you have because people like you, trust you, and want to support you. Anyone can use this type of power, which makes it both pervasive and the most easily abused. Personal authority can be the most important factor when others support your acts of intelligent disobedience. Use care when using personal power to influence others regarding acts of intelligent disobedience. Deploying personal authority ethically means that you must adhere to the following advice.

- Do not use *only* personal knowledge about individuals to influence them, by leveraging an individual's "hot buttons" or pain points. Ensure that you have a business basis for your influence. Discussions to influence others should be restricted to the benefits that the proposed act of intelligent disobedience provides to the business.

- Keep personal relationship dynamics outside of work-related discussions. Acts of intelligent disobedience at work should be treated as business issues – and only business issues. For example, if you know of a person who is highly disorganized when dealing with you outside of work, but who has demonstrated the opposite characteristic while in the office, it would be inappropriate to draw business conclusions based on your observations of that person outside of work. So if that person were to act with intelligent disobedience and bypass the typical organizational processes that would otherwise have been utilized, using your knowledge of their home life to conclude that they refused to put the effort in to be organized would not be ethical. Indeed, not only would it not be ethical, but it would also be detrimental to your personal authority, because it could erode trust. Base work judgments *only* on work-based observations.

Conclusion

Behaving ethically is a fundamental requirement for any role. However, acting with intelligent disobedience can challenge ethical norms. Awareness of corporate and geographical culture is critical when evaluating the ethical merit of a potential act of intelligent disobedience.

There aren't always clear right or wrong answers to whether a particular act of intelligent disobedience is ethical. This chapter provides guidelines that you can use to evaluate the ethics of intelligently disobedient approaches. A simple guideline is: if you have a nagging feeling about, or are unsure of, an action's ethical basis, you probably should refrain from taking that action. Alternatively, you can consider different approaches that you feel more comfortable about.

Take time to think, and, whenever possible, consider the implications of an act of intelligent disobedience before engaging.

Using intelligent disobedience should help you to sleep better, in the knowledge that you have done something to support your business. If you lose sleep instead, the reason for acting with intelligent disobedience is likely defeated.

Notes

1 Soltes, Eugene. 2017. Why it's so hard to train someone to make an ethical decision. *Harvard Business Review* [Online]. Available at: https://hbr.org/2017/01/why-its-so-hard-to-train-someone-to-make-an-ethical-decision [Accessed 16 February 2017].
2 Connors, Richard J. 2010. *Warren Buffett on Business: Principles from the Sage of Omaha*. Hoboken, NJ: John Wiley & Sons.

3 Biography. 2017. Edward Snowden: computer programmer [Online]. Available at: http://www.biography.com/people/edward-snowden-21262897#synopsis [Accessed 16 February 2017].

4 Smith, David, and Jacobs, Ben. 2017. Sally Yates fired by Trump after acting US attorney general defied travel ban. *The Guardian* [Online]. Available at: https://www. theguardian.com/us-news/2017/jan/30/justice-department-trump-immigration-acting-attorney-general-sally-yates [Accessed 16 February 2017].

5 John Adams Historical Society. 2017. John Adams, second president of the United States [Online]. Available at: http://www.john-adams-heritage.com [Accessed 27 August 2017].

Chapter 4

Simple and commonplace intelligent disobedience

You might assume that acts of intelligent disobedience are rare and always require significant amounts of courage. To the contrary: our society *relies* on intelligent disobedience to work efficiently and effectively. Seasoned and effective leaders use commonplace intelligent disobedience techniques frequently and smoothly – sometimes so smoothly that the techniques are taken for granted. These intelligent disobedience approaches are effective, and yet they can be leveraged without significant risk. This chapter explores several commonplace approaches to intelligent disobedience.

Society's reliance on intelligent disobedience

Probably the most pervasive reliance on intelligent disobedience applies to police officers performing their duties. We depend on the police to interpret the spirit, as well as the letter, of the law, for example not to enforce laws that are obsolete or nonsensical. Police should maintain law and order, while exercising reason and applying small doses of intelligent disobedience to ignore infractions when no danger exists or society is not adversely impacted.

This reliance on intelligent disobedience becomes obvious when police officers stage a protest. Imagine the effect on a city if police officers were to protest by strictly enforcing every law. People would be pulled over and fined for going 1 mile per hour above the speed limit, fined for jaywalking, or arrested for breaking obscure laws, such as the hideous crime of illegal use of a milk crate in Virginia.[1] All joking aside, the police could virtually shut down a town by applying the rule of law without consideration for the context and intent of those laws.

Examples of simple, quiet intelligent disobedience

Some of the most powerful acts of intelligent disobedience are executed quietly, without a lot of fanfare. Sometimes, only one or two people become aware of these actions. Yet simple acts of intelligent disobedience can be applied by managers in a wide variety of organizations, and can have significant and long-lasting impact on individuals and organizations. The stories in this section illustrate this quiet type of intelligent disobedience.

Example 1: deriving benefits in a nontraditional way

Attending IBM New Manager's School in 1984 after receiving my first managerial appointment is still vivid in my mind. I was excited, a bit overwhelmed with my new responsibilities, and anxious to ensure that I was "doing the right thing." One of the New Manager's School instructors brought in a hardback copy of IBM's manager's manual, which was a formidably large book. Upon dropping the book a few inches onto the desk to create an impressive noise, our instructor loudly declared:

> You need to understand everything that is in this book. However, if you look for answers from this book about what TO DO, I will be disappointed. Rather, I think you should look at a situation, understand the business objectives and our need to show respect for every individual. You then can decide what you think is the best action, and then use this book to ensure you aren't breaking the rules.

He didn't mean that literally for every managerial action we were to take, because the manual was rich with reasonable processes and procedures. His comment does convey the need to look at each business situation, to determine whether there are prescribed procedures involved, and then to do the right thing to get a favorable outcome. Akin to enforcing the law based on the spirit of that law, our instructor was encouraging us to use the manual in the way intended: to help us to become more effective managers.

Sometimes, we have to be a bit creative when bending the rules to address a given situation. Several months after my new manager training, I saw a manager demonstrate a very effective, yet small act of intelligent disobedience that reflected my instructor's approach. Over several weeks, a team of people made little progress resolving a difficult problem, until a colleague of mine came up with a novel idea. After several successful trials, the idea was implemented, with positive results. Instead of a standard award through a formal recognition program, my colleague's manager took a different approach to rewarding him. Knowing that he loved to travel and was an avid learner, the manager told my colleague to review the catalog of technical education offerings to find "a relevant course anywhere in the US that I can send you to."

The manager's manual said nothing about using the education program to reward an employee's performance nor did the recognition program say anything specifically about using education as a form of reward. Nothing prevented this, however, and it ended up being a great win–win application of existing programs. The business recognized an employee for outstanding work and benefited from a more capable employee with enhanced skills. The employee felt that he received excellent recognition for his effort, and was able to engage in his passion for travel and education. The unusual award created a memorable and lasting impression: my friend still talks about that recognition to this day, many years later.

Example 2: expanding your own responsibilities

Leaders in organizations frequently propose organizational changes and improvements. In project management, the initial document used to describe desired changes is called a "project charter." In change management circles, it is called a "change mandate." Regardless of the terminology, the leader who derives the idea or is assigned to design its implementation has an intelligently disobedient opportunity to take on additional responsibilities or authority to drive the desired change.

A project charter or similar document details the business opportunity or business problem to be solved and a high-level approach to achieving the desired outcomes, and *outlines the roles, responsibilities and authorities required* to implement the change. If you are writing, editing, or reviewing one of these documents, you have an opportunity to expand your responsibility and authority, if it makes sense, and can expedite the efficiency or effectiveness of guiding the change.

Consider the following example.

I was asked to design and manage the implementation of new application systems for a financial organization. My initial task was to draft the change mandate, which would be reviewed by the change management board, consisting of senior leaders in the organization. This change initiative had many stakeholders, including client support, the IT group, business areas that would need to deploy new business processes, and the contract management group. The contract managers were inexperienced in working with software vendors and application delivery contracts. Because this contract work would be a significant part of the change initiative, I saw their inexperience as a risk, but one that I could help to address. I believed that my experience working as an IT contract reviewer and negotiator would help the change initiative be more efficient and effective. But I did not want to cut the contracts team out of the process. In the draft change mandate, I assigned lead contract management responsibilities to myself, even though those responsibilities would normally rest with the contracts team.

When I circulated the document for review, I highlighted my proposal to take on the contract responsibilities. In addition, I personally reviewed the concept with the contracts manager, so that we could discuss his concerns and develop a high-level process for working together. After discussing his concerns, we agreed on how we could collaborate and effectively apply our collective skills. Other members of the change management board thought the proposal was a good idea and noted that they would not have thought of it themselves. Thus I received authority and responsibility that I would not likely have received otherwise, which helped me and the organization to work more efficiently.

Here are some guidelines if you are thinking of using this approach to expand your authority.

- Your increased responsibility should leverage the skills that you actually have, not your belief that you could do something better than the person doing it at present.
- You must clearly limit the extent and scope of your expanded responsibilities. In my example, I limited it to software vendor contracts in the single change initiative.
- You should consult with any managers whose areas might be affected or where responsibilities may shift to you from other people or departments.
- You must believe that the change in responsibilities or authority will genuinely help the organization to deliver outcomes more quickly or efficiently.

Encouraging skepticism

Many leaders seek to gain consensus and a unified front when engaging in a corporate initiative. To do that, though, they often consult only with those who agree with their proposal. Leaders who embrace intelligent disobedience seek out as many opinions and perspectives as possible. They want stories of failures, as well as successes. They encourage intuitive thoughts about how to succeed, as well as thoughts on how things could fail. Both optimism and pessimism are valuable, and should be nurtured to achieve the best results. The trick is ensuring that risks and ominous possibilities do not overwhelm the positive momentum you can gain from new approaches.

> " Leaders who embrace intelligent disobedience seek out as many opinions and perspectives as possible. "

Regardless of the approach you use, it's important to embrace both the optimists and skeptics in your organization – keeping things positive, while embracing team members who have lessons learned they want to share. This section describes some methods for achieving this balance.

Option 1: appointing a designated skeptic

People with skeptical viewpoints who still support your leadership and desired outcomes can be very valuable. You want them to express their views, but not at the expense of a valuable initiative or your team's performance. One approach is to formally appoint a supportive, concerned individual as the *designated skeptic*. You can give this person a regular time slot in meetings to discuss their concerns, along with potential remedies for the risks that surface. In this way, you show respect and appreciate the value of lessons learned, while preventing the skeptic from commandeering the conversation.

The designated skeptic may be an individual who has a tendency to identify risks. Alternatively, you can rotate the role from one team member to another, which encourages all members of your team to think of undesirable outcomes and potential remedial actions with which to avoid them.

Option 2: using resistance to identify new requirements

One of the most common forms of skepticism is individuals' resistance to change. This form of skepticism can create significant frustration. It can also be viewed as an asset to be embraced – particularly skepticism from leaders. Change resistance can be a valuable by-product from an organization that is being altered in some way. It can surface changes that provide a better result than the initial idea for the change.

Areas of resistance can potentially uncover new requirements for your change initiative. Keep in mind that resistance is a way of holding on to a value that is treasured. The key is to focus on sources of resistance that reflect a value that is still embraced by the organization at large. This resistance often produces ideas that support the cultural objectives of your initiative. On the other hand, you need to recognize resistance arising simply from fear of change in roles or processes, because that does not help to identify new requirements.

When many individuals resist a change for a common reason, it is time to listen. If people resist because they support traditional approaches that the organization feels are no longer useful, the change has not been sold well. You have a requirement to improve communication about the change. Listening to people's concerns will likely provide insight on how to make those improvements.

Consider this example of identifying requirements by analyzing resistance.

A team was replacing 25-year-old business processes and application systems with new processes and a specialized enterprise resource planning (ERP) system. The rank-and-file employees were concerned that additional data entry in the new ERP system would take longer and add pressure to their output targets. This was indeed true for the first time that they worked on a specific piece of equipment. After that initial data entry activity, however, they would work considerably faster, because the new ERP system would handle many tasks that they were currently doing manually. Once the management team recognized this resistance/skepticism, they prepared new examples to show how the new ERP system would work. As a result, team members were much more comfortable with the new approach.

Focusing on positive trends and the areas of most concern

Properly recognizing areas of risk or concerns with your team is important to gain buy-in and to drive positive outcomes. Holding regularly scheduled progress or planning meetings to track a change initiative is important, and they should focus on both the positive and negative aspects of your change. For example, you can ask each attendee to share what they believe is progressing well and what concerns them most. In this way, the team obtains a set of perspectives based on current information and their intuition. You can also use a risk register – that is, a log of items that may have an adverse effect on your change initiative – to supplement discussions or as a guide to avoid potentially negative consequences. The risk register will include actions to mitigate risks and serves as a "to do" list for the owners of any actions required to deploy those mitigations. By using a risk register, you can ensure that your discussions do not dwell only on risks or problems, but also focus on the solutions that can prevent those risks from becoming issues for your change initiative.

Moving from resistance to participation

After you have identified and used resistance to improve communication or to collect new requirements, it's time to convert that resistance to active participation. Ideally, ownership of a change initiative transfers from the leaders to a shared ownership by the leaders and team members.

A vital element of transferring ownership is communicating how a change will be implemented. Part of this communication is an element of counterintuitive intelligent disobedience: communicate that your change components *will not* deliver business value on their own. Rarely will a change initiative create deliverables that deliver business value by themselves. Instead, business value is realized only when team members use those new deliverables, and engage with them fully and purposefully.

Let me share an example to solidify this point.

The marketing leaders of a technical product company performed research, and concluded that a new sales focus would shorten their sales cycle and increase revenue. As a result, they created new sales collateral and a new deployment approach for their product. Initial reviews of the materials by prospective customers was overwhelmingly positive. Success was at hand! Or so they believed – for when the new sales collateral was distributed internationally, sales dropped.

What happened? The marketing leaders did not properly engage with the sales team. Their sales targets were not altered to allow them to participate in the educational sessions related to the new sales material and deployment method. Therefore few of the sales team members took the time to attend the education sessions, instead opting to teach themselves. The new sales and deployment approach, as described by the self-taught sales reps, was not received well by clients. Only when the sales team was appropriately educated and used the new deployment method properly did the anticipated sales improvement come to pass.

Using a deliverables map

One method to enhance communication to convert resistance to participation (such as that of the sales team, in the example) is to create a *deliverables map*, shown in Figure 4.1. These maps simplify communication with teams involved in a change initiative, and can also help to validate and solidify the approach taken by the leadership team.

The objective of a deliverables map is to clarify direction, breaking a complex change initiative down into simple steps. A good deliverables map will also detail the ownership of each step, so that team members understand their role in creating business value.

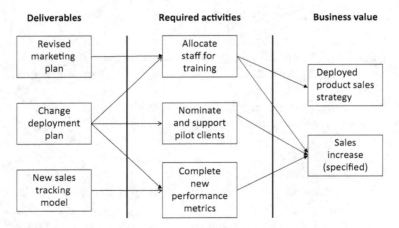

Figure 4.1 Deliverables map demonstrating activities required to convert deliverables from a change initiative into business value

In a deliverables map, the left-hand column contains a high-level list of the deliverables being produced to support a change initiative – in this case, the change in marketing and deployment methodology discussed in the previous example. The central column contains the activities that team members need to perform if business value is to be realized. The right-hand column depicts the business value to be achieved. Arrows between the boxes depict the relationships between the deliverables, the activities that team members must undertake, and the intended business outcomes to be achieved.

Here's another way to use resistance as an act of intelligent disobedience: you can contribute to an initiative's success by resisting working on an initiative that doesn't have a deliverables map (or a similar instrument) in place. A straightforward explanation of what an initiative is supposed to achieve and the corresponding activities required of employees is paramount to success. If a change initiative cannot be explained at a high level on a single page, such as in a deliverables map, then the chances of success are diminished. By demanding a deliverables map, you increase your organization's ability to succeed.

Doing the unexpected can yield substantial results

The simple act of doing something that people don't expect can be an effective application of intelligent disobedience. These unexpected acts are significant, yet are typically low-risk ways of getting results. Doing the unexpected can be especially effective when you need to contradict thoughts people have about your leadership, a change initiative, or expected behaviors from you or your leadership team. When people expect one thing and you do another, you have an opportunity to alter *other* expectations that you may wish to change.

> *The simple act of doing something that people don't expect can be an effective application of intelligent disobedience.*

Let me share an example.

I managed several outsourcing contract accounts for IBM. When an outsourcing engagement starts, emotions are high. Many people take on new roles. Others end up working for a new company, with no choice about being traded from their prior employer to an outsourcing company like IBM. They wonder what working for a new company will be like and what a new boss means to their careers. In many cases, some of their peers may have been laid off, which further increases emotion.

During the launch of one outsourcing engagement, all of these emotive factors were present – plus one more. The outsourcing contract called for improvements in performance against new quality targets. As employees newly transferred into IBM looked around, they saw most of the same people, sitting at the same desks, using the same tools they were using before the outsourcing contract was signed. People were scared that these improvements would be achieved by making people work harder, supporting unreasonable objectives. I understood that our new IBM employees assumed that the new IBM management team would be very conservative, and would be all business and no fun. I concluded that we needed to do something unexpected to start to change this perception before it led to negative attitudes.

I didn't want my action to be totally frivolous, but I certainly didn't want it to be "all business" either. I organized an indoor miniature golf tournament, with each of the 19 departments creating its own miniature golf hole. Along with their golf hole, each department was to create a poster that described what their department did and who their team members were. The overall team was large, spread over four buildings, so I required that everyone who played golf had to play all 19 holes, not only the holes in their building. Also, they had to create foursomes with people from four different departments. If someone did not want to play golf, they could watch, but I insisted that they also visit all four buildings to see all 19 holes. In addition, all department managers were to ensure that they supported on-call coverage for any business issues, so that everyone could "walk the course" to visit their colleagues and see the functions that each department performed.

It was interesting to watch as the tournament progressed. Many people had never visited the other buildings and did not know what their peers did. Many of the golf holes were creative and generated a lot of laughs. As I had hoped, the event ended up being a good team-building exercise, as well as demonstrating that the new IBM management team might not be "as evil" as expected.

More than once, I heard the phrase, "I didn't expect something like this." I had the opening I was hoping for! The event didn't change perceptions entirely to what I wanted them to be, but it did open up minds to different possibilities.

This unexpected action was not the end of the story nor would it be for any application of doing the unexpected. Minds may open up, breaking the mold of what is expected – but a new set of impressions needs to be imprinted on those newly opened minds.

I scheduled follow-on business activities to discuss how we were going to change processes for improved operational performance. My management team worked with their teams to determine what team members thought was helping them to do their jobs (so that we did not disrupt that) and what were the most significant obstacles to performing their jobs. We took that input to heart, combining the best of IBM's standard processes with the best of the processes used by our new colleagues. In the end, we deployed a cohesive set of processes that our team was comfortable executing.

Changing your tone

Speaking of simple ways to do the unexpected, try changing your tone of voice! I rarely raise my voice. In fact, I have a tendency to speak more slowly and in a monotone when tension is high. People I work with have become used to that. Should I change that approach and raise my voice, it gets attention.

I've come to realize that nobody actually hears *what* I'm saying when I raise my voice! They are so shocked to hear me yelling that what I say goes to the wayside. They think, "Wow, Bob must be *really* upset." That's the whole point . . . I purposefully say nothing particularly important when raising my voice. So I am prepared to repeat what I said in a calmer way. I use this technique very rarely, but, in my experience, it's 100 percent effective. If I believe that my team has become complacent about something and they potentially aren't listening because they have an expectation of what I will say or do, I raise my voice to kick their sense of urgency up a bit.

I have a colleague who is almost always boisterous. He changes his tone in the opposite way: he goes silent and stares at his team members. I think that really scares them! Once again, the change in tone – that small bit of doing the unexpected – can be powerful.

Should you decide to try this simple technique, remember: just like the miniature golf tournament, the act of behaving unexpectedly only sets the table for things to follow. It's what *follows* the unexpected act that makes the difference.

Note: The approach of changing your tone can easily be used to toy with people and play with their emotions. As with any act of intelligent disobedience, use this technique rarely and only for the greater good of the business, with a very specific business outcome in mind.

Conclusion

Acts of intelligent disobedience may be happening around us all the time. Intelligent disobedience can be executed by almost everyone in an organization, yielding great results when used properly, mindfully, and honestly. These simple tools and approaches are easily deployed and represent very little risk to you or your status within your organization. But you must use them properly, with business outcomes in mind, not as a means of needlessly exerting power over your colleagues.

Note

1 Justia. 2017. 2006 Code of Virginia §18.2–102.2: unauthorized use of dairy milk cases or milk crates; penalty [Online]. Available at: http://law.justia.com/codes/virginia/2006/toc1802000/18.2-102.2.html [Accessed 18 February 2017].

Chapter 5

Redefining courage

Intelligent disobedience is not for the meek. It requires balance and scrutiny. By performing those two tasks well, you and your team can consistently deploy acts of intelligent disobedience that yield positive outcomes. Courage is also required, but not always in a traditional sense. People who regularly act with intelligent disobedience rarely talk about "courage"; instead, they discuss "conviction," "fear of failure," "determination," or "following my intuition." Courage needs redefining when examining the inspirations for intelligent disobedience.

This chapter begins with motivations for engaging in intelligent disobedience. It also discusses how to assess your courage and risk profile relative to acting with intelligent disobedience. It provides tips for supporting courage and understanding the risk profiles of people in your organization. Finally, this chapter provides an assessment tool that can help you to decide whether to proceed with the act of intelligent disobedience that you're considering. Keep in mind that when and how to execute intelligent disobedience is a personal decision. No tool can predict with 100 percent accuracy whether you should perform an intelligently disobedient act.

A context for courage

Executing intelligent disobedience doesn't take the courage of Superman. It requires clear vision, strength of will, and the ability to face scrutiny regarding your actions and decisions. To understand this courage, examine the context in which you consider intelligent disobedience. This section outlines the elements that contribute to that context and then discusses each one in detail.

Any act of intelligent disobedience requires analysis before taking action. However, more extensive or "edgy" acts of intelligent disobedience require *significant* thought, because they can have both business and personal ramifications. Evaluate positive and negative ramifications, given your business and team goals, and what you are expected to deliver. More importantly, measure the benefits and risks relative to your own expectations. Your decision regarding intelligent disobedience can affect your career, the meaning drawn from your work, and your ethical balance. Before making those decisions, think about your courage and risk tolerance relative to:

- your ownership of the outcome(s);
- your desire to operate smartly in your role and environment;
- the professional and personal impact of the outcome, given the current approach, compared to an improved outcome resulting from an act of intelligent disobedience;
- your assessment of the potential and *realistic* impact on your family;
- your long-term view of the viability and desirability of continuing to work in your current role;
- your intuition about the potential action and outcome;
- your ability to conduct homework prior to acting;
- your personal view on the ethics of acting *or not acting* in the given business situation.

Healthy ownership of the outcome

Because acts of intelligent disobedience entail risk and require courage, you might not be motivated to act unless you feel strong ownership of the outcome of those acts. Healthy ownership of the outcome helps to motivate you to act wisely. However, some people take an unhealthy ownership of outcomes, which can lead to overstretching their sphere of influence or accepting excessive risk.

Suppose you designed a business process with an outcome that isn't coming to fruition. You'll likely feel a compelling need to act to help to achieve the outcome you envisioned. However, your ownership of the outcome is reduced if the process was launched by someone you don't know, if you don't have access to decision makers who control the process, or if your participation in the business process is virtually invisible. Yet some people will act even if they have no tangible ownership of the process or outcomes. These people need to be "solvers" to draw meaning from their work. Their personal approach is to identify and solve problems, find opportunities, and strive for the best outcomes, no matter what. If they believe that nobody else will step up to correct something, they feel compelled to do it themselves. This feeling of ownership may be appropriate at a point in time. However, it can linger in a way that isn't productive or healthy.

Consider an example of an unhealthy sense of ownership.

Many years ago, I changed jobs, yet I felt a compelling need to check in on my prior place of employment to ensure that all was going well. My ownership of the well-being of my former team prevailed in my thoughts, and I continued to try and support the team in the background. Not only did this ownership wear me down, but it also inhibited my former colleagues from building their own sense of ownership for their project. My former team needed to design their own business journey, and my ongoing expression of ownership created obstacles to that journey.

On the other hand, people driven by strong, healthy ownership will utilize intelligent disobedience actions without taking undue risks outside their sphere of influence. Healthy ownership comes from a balanced sense of responsibility, which involves balancing:

- your work and home life;
- your current and past responsibilities;
- your need to allow others to learn and grow through their own experiences;
- understanding that your approach may not be the only one that can succeed.

Generally, healthy ownership should be restricted to your current work duties. In addition, you should nurture and support healthy ownership displayed by people who work for you.

Recognizing and celebrating courageous intelligent disobedience

To ensure the appropriate execution of intelligent disobedience by your teams, it is important to recognize acts of intelligent disobedience. Even when you might have done something differently, a team member's reasonable action and appropriate acceptance of risk should be recognized and celebrated. If an adjustment to the intelligent disobedience is needed, you can help your team to become "more intelligent" in their disobedience by embracing their action as a learning opportunity. With that approach, you recognize your staff member's intention, while helping to fine-tune future acts of intelligent disobedience. Your tone and attitude during these discussions is crucial, because the prudence of selecting the next intelligently disobedient action will depend on how you approach this conversation.

Five items that you might focus on are as follows.

- What was your employee's overall intent?
- What are your specific concerns for the outcome, and what is your understanding of the belief or evidence that led your team member to act with intelligent disobedience?
- How did your employee discuss, analyze, or consider the circumstances prior to taking action?

- What type of communication followed the action, and what considerations for different, unintended outcomes were examined?
- How would you adjust the thought process for the next time this type of event occurs?

Remember: the goal is to strengthen your team member's sense of ownership by enhancing their intelligence toward the outcomes, constraints, opportunities, and risks that exist when considering acts of intelligent disobedience.

The desire to operate smartly

Professional growth is a strong motivator for many people, and intelligent disobedience that enhances outcomes stimulates professional growth. If you produce new and improved outcomes, you will become more valuable in your workplace, right? Not necessarily.

In their book, *Focus: Use Different Ways of Seeing the World for Success and Influence*,[1] authors Heidi Grant Halvorson, PhD, and E. Tory Higgins, PhD, talk about two types of person: those who are promotion-focused and those who are prevention-focused.

- Promotion-focused people look for new ways of achieving different outcomes and are willing to take risks when doing so.
- Prevention-focused individuals look to reduce any impacts from current outcomes to keep things flowing.

Both types are significantly motivated to engage in intelligent disobedience in the context of "operating smartly" in their own way of thinking. However, management's perceived need for each type of motivation can determine whether a disobedient act is viewed as intelligent.

Understanding whether you are motivated by promotion or prevention can help you to decide when to act and when not to act. You may be prematurely dismissing opportunities to achieve more stability if you are promotion-focused. Conversely, you may be overlooking ways of achieving incremental change and improvements if you are prevention-focused. How would management view your actions based on their desire for stability or change?

Working smartly may seem like common sense, but different staff members may interpret that common sense differently. If you manage others, understanding each team member's focus and supporting both promotion and prevention focus can expand your team's appropriate use of intelligent disobedience. Seek to understand and assess intelligent disobedience from both perspectives. By doing so, you encourage more courageous leadership from your team.

6 6 Positive business impact is the objective of intelligently disobedient actions. 9 9

Assessing business impact

Positive business impact is the objective of intelligently disobedient actions. The following are some guidelines for evaluating business impact to aid your decision making prior to acting with intelligent disobedience.

- What is the degree of overall impact (positive or negative) that the act will have on the business? Impact can be measured in monetary terms, in terms of perception by the marketplace, or in terms of its implications for a major client.
- What are the trade-offs between trying for improvement and being satisfied with the current outcome? Does striving for a better outcome add risk to an overall solution? If taking action to achieve a 95 percent solution could jeopardize the 80 percent you're already on course to achieve, that additional 15 percent might not be worth the risk.
- How much change is happening at the moment? The impact of people experiencing change fatigue can be significant. After going through periods of significant flux, people may not engage with a new initiative or won't appropriately apply intelligent disobedience because it requires more energy than they currently have. Being mindful of people's current capacity for change is important and involves foresight before you schedule more change. Consider your balance and the potential for change fatigue when you assess your courage or the courage of others.
- What is management's perception of your current success or improvement requirements? If they tell you you're too much of a risk taker, then acting with intelligent disobedience (whether or not the act is related to risks you have taken in the past) may not be prudent. Conversely, if they view your performance in a positive light, taking a risk by engaging in intelligent disobedience will be easier to manage with your superiors.

The *realistic* impact on you and your family

Taking risks is certainly easier when you have a healthy nest egg and your spouse earns a six-figure salary. Not all people have this luxury, so engaging in intelligent disobedience requires evaluating your feelings about potential negative outcomes. The following are some things to ponder when considering potential family impacts.

1   Will you really get fired for trying to improve business outcomes via an act of intelligent disobedience?

Some not-so-intelligent acts of disobedience (such as breaking the law or a government regulation) might merit termination of employment. However, it is unlikely that you would be fired because of acts of intelligent disobedience exercised under the guidelines put forth in this book. In workshop discussions, people sometimes start conversations with "I can't do that, I'd get fired." After some analysis and thinking through the actions of those of their colleagues who were fired, people develop more reasonable and accurate views of the implications of intelligent disobedience. The consequences of intelligent disobedience that doesn't go as planned are typically not as severe as people anticipate. Yes, an outcome may present some temporary, uncomfortable circumstances – but take care to ensure that you don't avoid acting with intelligent disobedience because of a greatly exaggerated fear of personal outcomes.

2   Would changing jobs be a major step backward because your current job is unique or particularly appealing?

Suppose that you feel the urge to engage in intelligent disobedience, but refrain from doing so because of realistic potential negative outcomes. In this situation, examine whether your comfort in your job is reasonable. Do you *really* have a great job if engaging in intelligent disobedience to create better outcomes would result in punishment? That seems more like a very discouraging place to be rather than an opportunity.

Some job situations (hours, location, skills required, and other factors) may suit you particularly well. Consider whether your desire for ownership, as discussed earlier in this chapter, is strong enough to outweigh the benefits of your current role. If it isn't, then you are likely to remain comfortable in your role even if you don't engage in intelligent disobedience. Otherwise, you should examine whether your role will truly provide you with an authentic work life.

3   Does your need for your work–life balance overshadow your desire or ability to engage in intelligent disobedience?

Consider factors such as working from home, supporting children or aging parents, and so on, when you evaluate whether to perform acts of intelligent disobedience. The additional work required before or after engaging in intelligent disobedience can be significant. Do you have the time for that in addition to your family responsibilities? Is your family situation temporary or long-term? If long-term and you do not have the ability to act with intelligent disobedience, will you become frustrated? If so, considering a job change may be warranted.

4   Do you have support from your management and colleagues to engage in the act of intelligent disobedience, which, over time, may enhance your career and the standard of living for your family?

Career advancement is another factor to weigh when considering intelligently disobedient actions. While appropriate acts of intelligent disobedience are meant to benefit the business, not the individual, people who successfully take action can and should benefit. People who consider engaging in acts of intelligent disobedience draw courage from the potential for advancing their career, which is entirely appropriate.

Evaluating flexibility in your current job

It is important to review what motivates you at work and to understand that flexibility to act with intelligent disobedience can significantly affect the meaning you get from your job. Summoning the courage to perform acts of intelligent disobedience is much harder if you don't have a degree of autonomy from your manager. This includes the ability to contribute to business goals and to face challenges by capitalizing on your views and capabilities.

Studies show that first-line management issues are the number one reason why people leave their jobs. There are other factors to job dissatisfaction, however, including a lack of challenge in your work activities, the ability to contribute to your organization's business goals, and autonomy and independence.[2] These factors reflect your ability to engage in intelligent disobedience! Acts of intelligent disobedience can often be challenging, utilizing a greater breadth of skills. Because they are geared toward achieving better business outcomes, they are intended to contribute to broader business goals. Engaging in intelligent disobedience is also a testimony to your ability to act with autonomy.

If you're reading this book, you're probably seeking ways of improving the outcomes of your business, your own approaches to work, or both. You may also be looking for different ways of leading others in a quest for better performance. Does your current job provide these opportunities to you? If you are a leader, do you provide these opportunities to your team via permission to engage in intelligent disobedience?

During the 18 years I worked for IBM, the best job and worst job I had were *the same job*. The change that occurred was a different manager. With that change came a significant reduction in autonomy and, in my perception, my ability to contribute to the goals of our organization. As a result, my management approach changed. With my previous manager, I deployed intelligent disobedience when

needed to make a positive impact; with my new manager, I had to spend significant time and effort to try to understand why I succeeded or generated fear in the
eyes of my new manager. I felt the need to engage in acts of intelligent disobedience to regain my autonomy rather than to advance business goals. My success
with these efforts was limited. Eventually, I concluded that my role was not viable
for me and pursued a different job. (Chapters 10 and 11 provide additional stories
of successful and not-so-successful intelligent disobedience.)

Your intuition

Valuing intuition is a trait shared by people who successfully perform intelligent disobedience. Because you won't always have time to evaluate situations,
your intuition may be the best barometer for determining whether you should
act. Because intuition is frequently triggered by unconscious memories of past
activities, your intuition is likely to be at least partially fact-based.

Your intuition should be a factor when guiding your employees concerning
acts of intelligent disobedience. Sometimes, you or your team will have the ability
to search for facts that validate intuition (the next section discusses doing this type
of homework). However, sometimes validation is not pragmatic, and intuition
will be your only guide. The vast majority of intelligent disobedience workshop
attendees say that following their intuition has resulted in significantly better outcomes. In contrast, regrets often resulted from disregarding intuitive thoughts.

Your ability to "do your homework"

"Doing your homework" prior to
engaging in intelligent disobedience
will increase your success. Doing
your homework and providing information to your team members to help
them to do their homework is a pru-

> " "Doing your homework" prior to engaging in intelligent disobedience will increase your success. "

dent way of managing the use of intelligent disobedience.

Homework can be general, relating to the overall culture of your organization
and its history with managing unusual situations versus executing standard processes. Homework can also be specific, such as understanding a given client, their
requirements, and the demands they place on your organization. For example,
altering standard processes for a client who is trying to exploit your team to get
out-of-scope services would not be wise.

Your personal view on ethics

As discussed in Chapter 3, your perception of the ethics of acting or not acting can outweigh every other factor when considering intelligent disobedience. Even so, it is prudent to evaluate the other factors in this section before you act. Even if these factors do not change your decision, thinking them through can solidify your confidence in your decision.

An intelligent disobedience decision model: assessing courage and risk

Deciding to engage in an act of intelligent disobedience is not like taking a test. Getting 65 percent to pass the test and ruling your act of intelligent disobedience to be prudent is not how things work. Business dynamics, relationships with management or your team, and shifting priorities are only a few factors that can vary from instance to instance. Because of that, it's risky to use any prescriptive tool for assessing whether intelligent disobedience is appropriate. However, using the factors presented in this chapter and applying a scoring model is useful in two ways:

- it facilitates a methodical approach to thinking through whether you should act with intelligent disobedience; and
- it provides information to reaffirm or question your intuitive certainty about acting with intelligent disobedience.

Here's how to use this tool.

1   Select the two topics that are most important to you (your vital topics). My inclination is to choose ethics and intuition as vital topics. I will not consider an act of intelligent disobedience if I rate the business impact topic as negative (my no-go criterion). Your mix of vital topics or no-go criteria may differ based on your current situation.
2   Rate each of the factors discussed in this chapter on a scale from +10 to −10 – where +10 indicates a situation conducive to engaging in intelligent disobedience and −10 detracts from your tendency to take action.
3   Multiply each of the ratings for your two vital topics by 3. By weighting the average, you take into consideration what is important to you at this particular time. Sometimes, you may be more sensitive to impacting your family, so you would weigh that topic more heavily.
4   Calculate the weighted average of all of the topics.

The following sections describe how to rate each of the factors.

Ownership

Using the +10 to −10 scale, rate the sense of ownership you feel for potential outcomes. Consider two factors: your personal sense of healthy ownership, and the sense of ownership that others – particularly your manager – feel you should have. If you and your manager are certain and passionate about your ownership of outcomes, rate ownership at +10. If you couldn't care less and your manager does not associate your actions with the outcomes under consideration, rate it at −10. If the situation is not at either endpoint, select a positive or negative rating that reflects your position within this continuum.

Desire

On the +10 to −10 scale, rate your desire for the type of outcome you seek (promotion or prevention). If you are a passionate promotion-focused person and the outcome is change or improvement, then you are aligned. In that case, rate desire at +10. The rating is also +10 when you are a highly prevention-focused person and the outcome you want to achieve is to retain current levels of performance. In contrast, if you are a strongly promotion-focused person and the action has a prevention-related outcome, the rating should be −10, because the outcome doesn't match your style. Ratings between the two endpoints can be affected by the degree of preference you have for promotion or prevention outcomes, and the nature of the outcome itself.

Note: Some outcomes can reflect both promotion and prevention, for example the outcome preserves the current process, while adding a new option path.

Business impact

Weigh the positive impacts of an act of intelligent disobedience against the risks for your business. If the potential benefits and risks are evenly balanced, rate business impact at 0. If your action produces all positive outcomes, set this rating at +10. If the act presents significant risk with minimal benefit, set this factor to −10. Realistically, +10 and −10 ratings in this area are rarely accurate. Your rating should weigh the benefits and risk in proportion to their probability and impact. For example, the risk may be a high probability and low impact; at the same time, the benefits might have a low probability, but would yield a significant improvement. Use your best judgment when selecting a rating for this area.

Realistic family impact

This rating represents the impact on your family that may result from engaging in intelligent disobedience. Similar to business impact, 0 represents a balance between benefit and risk, and the +10 and −10 ratings are all benefit and all risk, respectively. Again, a rating of +10 or −10 is rare in this area. For this rating, you should assess the time the act might take away from family, your family's current need for support, and their support (or lack of support) for your career aspirations.

Viability of your current role

If you are supported in your role, enjoy what you are doing, and foresee ongoing happy employment, you are all in with your company and can rate viability at +10. If you are actively looking for another job and dread going to work each day, you aren't invested in your job and should rate this factor at –10. In between, select a rating that reflects your position within this scale.

Intuition

This rating represents the degree to which your intuition is triggered. A rating of +10 means that your intuition is screaming for action, while –10 means that your intuition warns you to refrain from acting. Otherwise, select a positive or negative rating that reflects your position within this scale.

Homework

This rating is relevant only when you are planning an act of intelligent disobedience in advance. Rate this factor at +10 when you have time and access to information, and you validate the intelligently disobedient action with your manager and colleagues. If no information is available and you do not have access to colleagues and your manager prior to deciding on your action, you are on your own and should set this factor at –10. The availability of people with whom you can talk or the extent of information that's available will determine your position on the +10/–10 continuum.

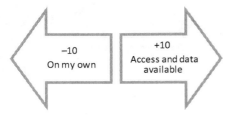

Ethics

This rating represents the degree to which you feel compelled to act based on your personal ethical makeup. For this rating, you should also consider the ethical perspectives of your colleagues and management team. If you and your managers or colleagues agree that ethics dictate action, set this rating as positive, up to +10. If you and your managers or colleagues agree that ethics indicate no action, set this factor as negative, up to −10. In contrast, if your ethics are not in alignment with those of your management team or colleagues, then the rating should move toward 0.

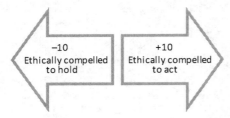

An example of scoring

Table 5.1 is an example of scoring an assessment in which intuition and ethics are the vital topics. Table 5.2 is a blank scoring model for your own use when assessing your own intelligent disobedience actions.

Table 5.1 Example of a completed score sheet when using the intelligent disobedience decision model

Factor	Rating	Weighted rating
Ownership	8	8
Desire	7	7
Business impact	6	6
Realistic family impact	4	4
Viability of role	7	7
Intuition	8 × 3	24
Homework	5	5
Ethics	9 × 3	45
Total rating.		**106**
Weighted average		**106 ÷ 12 = 8.83**

Note: Divide the total by the number of weighted topics. There are eight topics, but the two vital topics are weighted by three, so the total number of weighted topics is 12.

Table 5.2 Blank score sheet for use with the intelligent disobedience decision model

Factor	Rating (−10/+10)	Vital factor (choose two and multiply those scores by 3)	Weighted rating
Ownership			
Desire			
Business impact			
Realistic family impact			
Viability of role			
Intuition			
Homework			
Ethics			
Total			
Weighted average			

The weighted average of 8.83 in Table 5.1 is a relatively strong indicator that the intelligently disobedient action under consideration should be taken. If your assessment includes conflicting responses (such as highly positive for business impact and highly negative for family impact), pause and consider the broader and longer-term implications of the proposed action.

Conclusion

This chapter provided some perspectives to consider when contemplating an act of intelligent disobedience. It doesn't provide a definitive and comprehensive formula for determining action – for that involves more variables than can be addressed in a book targeting a diverse population.

Notes

1 Grant Halverson, Heidi, and Higgins, E. Tory. 2013. *Focus: Use Different Ways of Seeing the World For Success and Influence*. New York: Hudson Street Press.
2 Heathfield, Susan M. 2016. Top 10 reasons why employees quit their jobs [Online]. *The Balance*. Available at: https://www.thebalance.com/top-reasons-why-employees-quit-their-job-1918985 [Accessed 30 March 2017].

Chapter 6

History is rarely made by the well behaved

Successful intelligent disobedience often requires nonstandard behavior – in other words, acts that don't fall into the "well behaved" category. This chapter examines different forms that intelligent disobedience can take, such as: bending rules, breaking rules, or inventing rules to suit a given situation; or challenging the decisions of individuals, a group, or external entities. These actions may be visible to many, a few, or only the person taking action. The examples in this chapter are not actions executed by people being well behaved or blending in with the average manager or employee.

Following the rules with intelligent disobedience

In the following scenario, a manager *followed* the rules as a means of executing intelligent disobedience.

Phil managed an IT group for a government agency. The group was to be outsourced, and his team was reduced to a skeleton crew by means of retirements, transfers, and voluntary layoffs. Data centers were scheduled to be consolidated just prior to the outsourcing, which would require extensive preparation and weekend work from staff members who would not have a job after the consolidation was completed.

Phil maintained excellent relationships and worked well with his team. Even so, keeping staff focused was a challenge. The data center work was going to be complicated and was made more difficult because Phil's agency had placed a moratorium on paying overtime. To avoid outages during business hours, performing work on the weekend was the only alternative. Phil believed that the consolidations were unlikely to be successful if the people assigned (who would soon lose their jobs) were not paid overtime.

Phil applied for an exception to the overtime moratorium, which was denied. He appealed, to try to overturn that decision, and was denied again. Exasperated,

Phil wondered how he could find incentives to get his team members to go beyond their job scope and hours to complete the consolidation.

The fact that his team needed to go beyond their normal job scope gave Phil an idea. He consulted with HR and confirmed his ability to post new positions. The minimum time for which he needed to advertise a new job before he filled it was one week. He also verified that no minimum duration was needed for a new role.

Phil defined new roles for the four key staff members spearheading the data center activity. He posted the new roles and advertised them, so that anyone could apply – but the duration of the roles was only five weeks. Not surprisingly, only those people who were currently on Phil's team applied. Their qualifications were reviewed and accepted. As a result, Phil's team members received promotions and higher pay for the remaining five weeks of their employment. Out of appreciation for Phil's efforts, the team completed the data center consolidation without a hitch.

Despite the positive outcome, the agency reviewed Phil's approach. Based on an audit of his hiring process, the agency issued a findings letter, which stated that the "hiring process was not defensibly fair and open, but that overall the processes followed were consistent with the principles in the organizational guidelines." The letter continued with a specific review of Phil's performance, stating:

> Management has reviewed your performance, and we have decided there should be no adjustment to your bonus pay. In assessing your performance against your agreement for next year, however, we will place particular attention on the need for appropriate management practices.

One could argue whether the note says that Phil behaved properly. In the end, no true penalty was levied. In addition, in future job interviews, his "appropriate management practices" did not deter hiring managers; they actually enhanced Phil's career options.

Showing up can constitute intelligent disobedience

"Must be present to win" was a concept embraced by Sylvia, who earned a new job by being in the right place and presenting herself as confident and capable.

Sylvia moved to a new city without a job. After scanning job postings for several weeks, Sylvia changed her approach. She wanted a role as a financial analyst and aspired to work for a company she admired. Because she had not seen job openings posted by that company, she decided to be proactive.

Sylvia was confident that a few minutes with a decision maker would earn her an informational interview and maybe something more substantial. She decided to engage in intelligently disobedient behavior and go on a "scouting mission" to improve her chances of landing a desirable job.

She decided to visit a satellite office of her favored company, because she thought that the chances of a useful, informal discussion were greater in a smaller local setting. She walked into the office and found the finance department listed on the lobby directory. There was no security in the building lobby, so she proceeded to the front desk of the department.

Smiling, Sylvia said that she was there for an interview for the financial analyst job. Confused, the person at the desk asked Sylvia to wait and disappeared into the office. After a few minutes, the receptionist returned and apologized, saying they didn't know their job request had been approved, so they were unaware she was coming. However, if she could return in 30 minutes, the receptionist's boss would interview her at that time. Thirty minutes later, Sylvia had a very positive and productive conversation with the department manager about the opening in his department.

The next morning, Sylvia called and confessed that she had "popped in" with hopes of getting information on work possibilities. Karl, the department manager, laughed and said, "Well, that explains things." When Sylvia apologized, Karl said:

> Don't you dare! I appreciate someone with initiative, and I think your skill set is just what we need. HR said they approved my role today, so I will be interviewing other people. I think you are a strong candidate, and I will contact you in a couple of weeks.

Ten days later, Karl called and offered Sylvia the job.

Let's examine this story further.

Sylvia was acting in her personal interest in finding a job. She did not work for an organization that would benefit from her intelligently disobedient behavior. However, her intent was to get a job so that she *and* the company would benefit: she did not make up her qualifications. She took the initiative to show up for a job interview in the hopes that she might land one, and she quickly confessed the true nature of her visit. Ultimately, she made a significant contribution, working for the company for eight years in increasingly challenging roles. The outcome was positive for everyone involved.

Changing the game: "badge in the box" meetings

Corporate culture is a key factor affecting the ability to engage in intelligent disobedience. When challenging the decisions or ideas of senior leaders is frowned upon, executing intelligent dis- obedience can be very difficult. In cultures like this, compliance and not "stirring the pot" is expected, regardless of whether it is produc- tive.

> *Corporate culture is a key factor affecting the ability to engage in intelligent disobedience.*

Venturing outside the lines is considered bad behavior.

Sam encountered this type of environment upon joining a well-established, growing manufacturing company as its chief operating officer. Reinforcement of the hierarchy was everywhere: on posters, in the layout of management offices, and via clearly designated parking spots. Boldly printed signage dissuaded non-managers from straying into coveted management parking spaces. Employee badges had different background colors, distinguishing managers from non-managers. All managers had administrative assistants, who carefully managed their bosses' calendars.

Sam was unhappy with this hierarchical environment. He had learned from his initial staff interviews that his non-management team members were discouraged from speaking up. He also knew that establishing trust to share ideas was the only way of fully leveraging his team's expertise.

Sam needed to acknowledge the existing culture, while also encouraging challenges to long-held business practices. To accomplish those goals, Sam invented "badge in the box" meetings. At these meetings, all ideas and constructive criticism of existing practices was encouraged. To reinforce this openness, which was unfamiliar to his staff, Sam sent invitations to the meetings himself and arrived at the conference room first. He would hold a box, so that everyone entering the room could put their badges (the reinforcers of the organizational hierarchy) into the box. Sam would then outline the rules for the meeting, as follows.

1   While badges are in the box, there is no hierarchy. We are people with ideas and skills, with an opportunity to improve the business.
2   Everyone gets a chance to speak, nothing is out of bounds, and no minutes will be kept for the meeting while badges are in the box.
3   Flip charts will be used to capture and confirm any ideas that are discussed. No flip chart will leave the room unless all attendees believe that it represents what was discussed and is favorable for the business.

It required a couple of these meetings before Sam felt that his team had the confidence to share their perspectives without "sugar coating."

However, Sam believes that the meetings led to immediate improvements. He attributes the change to the "badge in the box" approach, which recognized the corporate culture and its weakness. Suppressing ideas and preventing open discussion took energy out of staff members. Without his intervention, getting to know his staff would have been difficult and time-consuming. The meetings represented intelligently disobedient behavior by breaking down the toxicity in his corporate environment, while not significantly disrespecting the organization's culture.

Not taking action can be intelligent disobedience

Sometimes, engaging in intelligent disobedience means doing (almost) nothing at all. Here's an example.

I was asked to manage a department that was in considerable distress. The company had just completed its annual employee survey to collect views and opinions from staff. The anonymous survey asked questions in four categories: job content, clarity and frequency of company communications, working conditions, and views on first-line management. The results were rolled up by department, division, and the overall company. From this data, the company calculated an overall employee satisfaction score, in addition to scores for each of the four categories. The scores were represented as "% positive," where neutral choices were not considered positive. The department I was asked to manage had scored its first-line manager at "0% positive," meaning that all 16 people in the department had rated their first-line manager at neutral, negative, or strongly negative for *every* question. In addition, they scored working conditions very low. The senior management team was very concerned, concluding that the department was "severely broken." They asked me to develop an extensive set of action plans to correct the situation.

Understanding the department members' perception of the situation was paramount. I scheduled interviews with each staff member in a relaxed atmosphere: the company canteen or a casual cafe. I listened to each employee's story and sources of concern. The team provided considerable input, with great consistency in their views. Their former manager had a brilliant technical mind, but he had trouble letting his employees tackle tasks independently. Their concern was very straightforward: their former manager wasn't letting them do their job their way. As a result, they didn't feel valued.

No significant action plans were required to recover this department; the team members simply needed to be left alone to do their work and be recognized for their contributions. Putting an extensive set of action plans in place would have been disastrous. That approach would have indicated to the department members that they were the problem and needed fixing.

I defied the direction given to me by my management and attended my survey action plan review meeting with four short action items.

1   Together, each employee and I would define the technical requirements for their output. When those conditions were met, their output would be considered acceptable.
2   The organization's standard high-level approaches would be applied to work produced. No further process direction would be given by management, unless department members asked specific questions or outputs were not acceptable.
3   The department team leaders, who coordinated work for their areas, would assign and evaluate all output. As the department manager, I would be consulted only when guideline interpretation was required or when process questions surfaced between our group and other departments.
4   An offsite meeting with second-line management would be held at the end of each month to provide feedback on progress.

These four action items failed to impress my senior managers. They asked why "only these actions" would heal an unproductive department that felt so dissatisfied. My reply was that a fundamental tenet of employee satisfaction had been violated: employees need to feel valued and perceived as having legitimate skills to contribute. The remainder of what needed to happen was to fulfill the responsibilities of a first-line manager – that is, providing HR administration and guidance when circumstances warranted. Hesitantly, management let me proceed with my four action items. After two senior management meetings with the team, management was satisfied that the department was healing sufficiently and that productivity was improving.

I spoke to my predecessor in the role. He believed that his process and technique support was helpful, and was distraught with the result of the survey. He concluded that, sometimes, *not* helping and instead focusing on what people need or expect from their manager provides the best outcome.

Fulfilling your responsibilities as a form of intelligent disobedience

Leaders are often asked to provide stewardship for a project or to direct some form of organizational change. It is wise to work with senior management to define stewardship or sponsorship responsibilities and the responsibilities you delegate to your team. This sharing of responsibility ensures that the best skills are deployed, while maintaining appropriate guidance and management for the project. Beyond management of metrics, stewardship of a project involves protecting your team from the pervasive conflicts and politics in organizations. It also involves challenging management when required.

Kevin embraced this responsibility set while serving as a project sponsor in an entertainment services company. Overall business success inspired lofty ambitions among the company's senior management team, and they launched a large portfolio of projects without sufficient prioritization or resource management. Projects competed for scarce resources, and stress levels increased across the business.

Kevin needed to act to protect his project. Reviewing his sponsorship role, he noted that his responsibilities included "addressing any issues or hurdles that could hamper project progress." With that responsibility in mind, Kevin chose to challenge his senior leader, who was on the portfolio management board, stating that the manager was approving too many projects. Kevin began the conversation by confirming his role as the chief of stewardship for the project and the resulting business outcomes. He also confirmed his responsibility to diligently work to eliminate obstacles or mitigate risks on the project. After those affirmations, he continued, "I am here to both eliminate an obstacle and mitigate some personnel risks for my project. You need to stop putting more projects in the pipeline! My project's biggest obstacle and risk is *you*!"

Because he had a good relationship with his manager, Kevin could deploy such direct communication. By first confirming his responsibilities, Kevin could more easily commit the act of intelligent disobedience to challenge his manager's decisions. Kevin did not expect other projects to be rejected or suspended. However, he intended his challenge to draw focus to a pervasive issue. He then made the following observations and recommendations.

- The lack of project priority had led critical team members to change direction and focus, reducing their productivity and making project scheduling difficult. Missed deadlines plagued the organization, reducing trust between project teams and their business customers.
- Time was wasted on administration, taking time away from achieving outcomes. Kevin's project team spent inordinate time changing project schedules, because task completion forecasts changed almost every week when key staff members were redirected to work on other initiatives. Stabilizing resource assignments was necessary to increase productivity.
- Project outcomes needed to be prioritized, so that Kevin and his fellow project sponsors could prioritize staff time and produce realistic schedules. Priorities would also reduce staff stress and further increase productivity, because staff could concentrate on fewer, high-priority items. It would also facilitate effective change management planning: realistic schedules were necessary to determine when project deliverables would be ready to integrate into the business environment.

Not many projects were put on hold, as Kevin expected. However, the intelligently disobedient conversation that he had with his senior leader slowed the approval of future projects, which led to better outcomes for his business.

Cancel an initiative, and disregard the money you have spent

Crystal balls are far from flawless, which is why acts of intelligent disobedience are so vital to drive optimal business outcomes. Inaccurate foresight can apply to single business decisions or individual department processes. Larger initiatives, such as significant projects, new product development exercises, or changes in business direction, can also suffer from lack of vision and go astray. Business changes, skill mismatches, loss of key staff, inappropriate planning, or ineffective project sponsorship are a few of the issues that can spoil well-conceived plans and create issues with major initiatives.

One of the most significant and important acts of intelligent disobedience is the cancellation of a business initiative that is no longer *66 Leaders exercising intelligent disobedience decisively cancel initiatives 99*
productive. However, the key is to not have a "hair trigger" and kill business initiatives as soon as things go bad. Leaders exercising intelligent disobedience decisively cancel initiatives, but not without diligently performing the following analyses.

1   Disregard the sunk costs (money already spent on an initiative), and instead focus on the return on investment of the *next dollar* that will be spent.

What has been spent so far probably cannot be clawed back. Focus should be placed on accomplishments thus far, and on the issues and risks to overcome to ensure that additional money spent will yield results. If a viable plan to address issues is available, proceed to the next item in this list. If not, intelligent disobedience values protecting the upcoming dollars to be spent rather than pushing on simply because "some outcome" is desired from the money spent thus far.

2   Determine whether the original intent of the initiative is still valid.

Often, initiatives take a circuitous path: scope changes or expands, and the original intent of your organization's efforts is lost. Is the current work geared toward a different, unclear, and not universally understood set of objectives? Carefully scrutinize initiatives demonstrating this symptom, for it is a warning sign of potential project failure.

3   Determine whether the customer is engaged and dedicating significant resources (in numbers or key skills) to drive this initiative to completion. If not, spending more money and time on the initiative will not yield positive results.

Courageously cancelling initiatives can represent a proactive alternative to complete failure. Intelligently disobedient leaders cancel initiatives – but only after carefully combing through all of the work done for items that might be redeployed elsewhere or which serve as valuable lessons learned for future projects.

Intelligent disobedience through relentless persistence

Belief systems inspire a sense of belonging to an organization or partnership and are an important part of motivation. Whether a partnership is personal, between businesses, or amongst a team, outcomes driven by shared values and enhanced by persistence can produce profound results and inspire fierce loyalty for the leader or amongst the partners.

The following two stories are examples of persistence that produced these outcomes.

Example 1: Suzie and Norman

The persistence of Suzie and her husband led to a long and happy marriage. First, their persistence helped them with the decision to get married. Suzie's husband, Norman, was persistent, repeatedly asking her to marry him every few months. Suzie, equally persistent, would reply "no," citing differences regarding managing finances and future plans that they needed to resolve. Norman's persistence did not frustrate Suzie, she explained, because it assured her that he genuinely wanted to share his life with her.

Suzie was concerned about her own persistence, however. Deep down, she wanted to get married – but only if she felt comfortable that they were aligned on important life matters. She also did not want Norman to get discouraged.

Suzie decided to change her tactic without compromising her beliefs or her desire to align their views. The next time Norman proposed to her, she exercised intelligent disobedience by replying "yes, with conditions." Norman was elated, then stepped back when he absorbed what Suzie had said.

Suzie laid out her recommendations for how they should manage finances and plan their future. While Norman didn't accept her recommendations initially, they both were energized by the conditional acceptance of the marriage proposal. Persistence continued to be their approach. Two months after Suzie's conditional proposal acceptance, she accepted formally and they notified their friends. That, shared Suzie, was 15 years ago, and they continue to work with persistence to come to agreements they are fully happy with before finalizing their decisions.

Example 2: Alfredo

Alfredo Castillo was serving his country in Iraq. His persistence enhanced a bond and generated pride for an entire fighting unit. Alfredo was always moved by the image of his high school bulldog mascot. He was so enamored of it that he shared the image with his fellow soldiers and wrote to his *alma mater*, receiving permission to use the bulldog image on his brigade's equipment. The soldiers painted the mascot on all of the Humvee transport vehicles, plainly visible to friend and foe.

Fearing unwanted issues, Castillo's brigade commander ordered all of the bulldog images be removed. The soldiers refrained from removing the images. In a rare case of resistance to command, they persistently lobbied for the bulldog to remain on their equipment. Seeing the degree of pride and solidarity that the image conveyed for his troops, the commander relented, and the mascot was allowed to remain on their vehicles. The soldiers used the bulldog image as their rallying point and shared their enthusiasm for the emblem with the Iraqi people whom they were assisting. The bulldog became a symbol of hope and support for many Iraqis, and a reinforcing source of energy for a brigade that had been struggling with its long and arduous mission.

Conclusion

Intelligent disobedience and doing what is expected rarely go hand in hand. However, widely radical or creative ideas aren't necessarily needed to successfully act with intelligent disobedience. Fundamental approaches, such as looking at ways of deploying the rules differently, challenging assumptions about how people act or think, making subtle adjustments to manage corporate culture, or simply being persistent, are refined ways in which to effectively deploy intelligent disobedience.

Chapter 7

Share the truth

Intelligent disobedience is based on truth. Truth is not universal, so you need to consider truth carefully to ensure that your disobedience is intelligent. A truth that is straightforward from your perspective may appear totally different to someone with other experiences and cultural background. This chapter examines truth within the context of intelligent disobedience. It also describes tactics that you can employ to search for truth. Also discussed is whether lying is a valid approach when engaging in intelligent disobedience. It provides approaches for collecting truth and sharing it with challenging leaders.

A perspective on truth

Because of widely diverse family, spiritual, education, and business backgrounds, everyone has a different perspective of "the truth." In her fabulous book, *Fierce Conversations*,[1] author Susan Scott examines the concept of truth. Truth, she proposes, is owned by the entire organization rather than by any individual. For example, what might be a simple exercise to one person can be difficult to another. A person who is very approachable to one employee could be terrifying to someone else.

To make the best decisions regarding intelligent disobedience, it's important to recognize that a broad range of perspectives may be present. When exercising intelligent disobedience, don't mistake *your* truth for *the* truth. "The truth" is a broader set of truths brought to the table by the people around you.

Collecting truths

The case study of Edward Snowden in Chapter 3 involves a considerable assumption about truths. Snowden professed a strong belief in relation to whether collecting information about individuals was right or wrong – but did he have any information about what the public thought about that? For example, would the majority of Americans approve the surveillance he witnessed if they were to feel that it protected them from terrorism? The ability to collect public perceptions about surveillance would make it easier to assess whether Snowden's actions were indeed "intelligent" disobedience. His situation has become even more tenuous because of people's truths: his living in Russia (at the time of writing) to avoid arrest in the United States has raised concerns about possible ties to Russian intelligence services.[2]

Although your acts of intelligent disobedience might not have as broad-reaching implications as the Snowden case, collecting truths prior to acting with intelligent disobedience is still important for building positive perceptions. Collecting truths will make your intelligent disobedience more successful and increase your support from management, peers, and the team members you lead.

The key is to ask for truths from others and provide an environment in which to share those truths safely and completely. Explain the intended outcome of your act of intelligent disobedience before you ask people to share their truths with you. Because truths might reveal emotions, fears, or past experiences that aren't public knowledge, people rarely risk sharing their truth without seeing some benefit. Make sure that your benefit descriptions are crisp and relevant to the people whom you ask to share their truths.

In addition, use the following guidelines when collecting truths.

- Don't listen to truths and walk away without confirming your understanding of what you heard. To ensure that you understand, paraphrase what you heard, using examples and specific scenarios.
- Link the input you receive to the sender's potential benefit or concern.
- When appropriate, share the collected truths you receive with the entire group of people who contributed them.
- Let people know if you decided to act (or not act), why, and the resulting outcome.
- Express appreciation to all who shared truths and do not use the information shared inappropriately. (See Chapter 3 on using power ethically.)

Share truth universally – even with tough customers

Harry had a reputation as a "tough customer" – in fact, one of my employer's toughest customers. A voracious reader, with an incredible ability to deduce what was happening from seemingly disparate facts, Harry intimidated most people. Warnings were plentiful for people scheduled to present to Harry:

- answer his questions and only those questions;
- do not speculate or share any distinct action plans, because he will pull them apart and micro-manage you;
- speak carefully and don't make specific commitments, because he'll remember every word you say and hold you to account;
- don't challenge him in a public setting, because he will make your life quite unpleasant if you do so.

In essence, the advice was to share truths sparingly.

Working with Harry was not something that people looked forward to. In fact, some employees literally recoiled in terror when having to deliver news to Harry. He was smart, driven, and razor-sharp. Mix in a bit of paranoia and a penchant for loudly sharing his opinions without sugar coating, and it was no surprise that he inspired fear.

My organization's lack of success with working with Harry called for a different approach. In a blatant act of disobedience that I hoped was intelligent, I discarded all of the advice I'd been given about working with him.

During his weekly status meetings, which I attended, Harry's reputation was on full display. Loud, critical, sarcastic, and quite succinct in his observations, he was adept at putting people to the test. He readily detected doubt and any lack of clarity in responses. Harry desperately sought truth. Viewing himself as captain of a ship, he wanted information on the status of his vessel – that is, the business unit he managed. He wanted information to establish a direction and understand the improvement plans for his organization. However, because of his behavior, people did not provide information readily, especially in areas with technical struggles or for projects that were behind schedule.

The different approach I chose was to "open the books" and share all of the information I had about what my team was doing. I approached Harry and said, "I want to share some activities you aren't hearing about in status meetings, so I can hear your views and opinions." That piqued Harry's interest. He said, "The best time for quiet discussion, without distractions, is at 6.30 am, when I first get to the office. Meet me there tomorrow morning."

Whether it was the early-morning quiet, the fact that I had introduced the agenda as an opportunity to share, or both, Harry's demeanor was entirely different the next day. I requested permission to share honestly, confessing that my management team might not be totally comfortable with what I intended to share. I asked him to respect the risk I was taking with my management and to treat the information appropriately. He gave me his word, with an expression on his face that I had not seen before. That gave me confidence that I was doing the right thing.

I shared what I thought was going well and why. I also shared the areas in which I thought improvement was needed, which ones I had prioritized, and the ones I would address first. Lastly, I made suggestions about how I could share status for initiatives during our weekly status meetings with the entire management team and also how I could share supplementary information with him informally outside of those meetings. Harry agreed and we ended our discussion.

From that point forward, my relationship with Harry changed. Status meetings that included my senior manager were often still rough, and Harry would still call me out for things he was unhappy with. However, he consistently supported me and applauded my diligence in separate discussions he had with my management team. He was open to suggestions on what he could change to help my team to achieve better outcomes.

Over the course of a year, Harry and I had seven or eight of those early-morning discussions. I scheduled about two-thirds of them; Harry, the others. At no time did Harry use the informal status information I provided – the truths he wanted to understand – as leverage against me. In fact, he did just the opposite – giving me the benefit of the doubt when things weren't turning out as planned. *Harry just wanted the truth.* To this day, many years later, I know he will oblige if I ask for a favor, as I will for him.

Not all people react like Harry when presented with truths; some may use that truth against you. However, taking the inherent risk to openly share the truth is a fundamental element of intelligent disobedience. If you're concerned that your counterpart might betray the truths you

> *taking the inherent risk to openly share the truth is a fundamental element of intelligent disobedience.*

share, consider having a candid discussion about what you are doing. If you don't receive reassurance that the truth will not be weaponized in the future, you have no motivation to continue to share truths. Give your counterpart a choice: treat shared truths appropriately, or face management decisions and situations with partial information, and deal with the inefficiency that may bring.

Harry's story provides two lessons.

- Find the core truths needed by someone who may be difficult to manage. Satisfy that need – even if it means engaging in intelligent disobedience – and your stakeholder management job will be easier.
- Work with your difficult customer to determine the time and approach to take to generate the most productive conversations. In Harry's case, that was in his office, one-on-one, at 6.30 am. Another senior manager whom I worked with

would take an hour-long walk, twice a week, to smoke a cigar and reflect. That was a great time for an in-depth conversation with him. Some people don't clearly define the time and circumstance for productive conversations. In those cases, trial and error is necessary; try to schedule future conversations at times and circumstances similar to those of your previous successful conversations. Lastly, use these "precious times" cautiously. You do not want to overstay your welcome and intrude on time that may otherwise be focused on issues that don't involve you. Ask for these meetings only when significant items are at stake.

Sharing the whole truth

With Harry, intelligent disobedience involved sharing whole truths. Could sharing only *part* of the truth be a legitimate and ethical form of intelligent disobedience? The answer lies in the intent and transparency of the action.

Some people get bogged down in detail and are easily distracted by items that shouldn't concern them. Sometimes, the best intelligent disobedience action is to hold back truths that could distract people and to put desired outcomes at risk. This can become a slippery slope, however. Remember: the truth does not belong only to you! If you withhold bits of truth from your leaders and those bits find their way to them via other means, you could damage a trust-based relationship.

The following are some options to consider in relation to sharing parts of the truth.

- Obtain agreement from your leaders in advance about which detailed truths do not need to be shared. For instance, your manager may want to know only whether you are forecast to be on budget at the end of the fiscal year; the fact that you are achieving that goal by reallocating funding from one business area to another may or may not be of interest. Before holding back information, determine the threshold or areas in which your manager expects to receive full details. You may find that your manager wants to know whether you shift more than 10 percent of your budget or that a particular area of your business will be subject to funding changes. While this may seem to restrict your ability to engage in intelligent disobedience, you will know your manager's sensitivities – vital homework to ensure that your manager views any disobedience as intelligent.
- Share the full truth *after* the event. This approach is a version of asking for forgiveness rather than permission. It helps to preserve trust, while giving you the opportunity to understand your manager's boundaries and sensitivities. If your manager responds negatively to this approach, do not repeat it. Doing so could significantly and permanently erode trust.

- Go for it, and share only the relevant truths, leaving details out unless specifically asked. I recommend reviewing the intelligent disobedience decision model from Chapter 5 to evaluate whether acting with intelligent disobedience in this manner is prudent.

Lying as an act of intelligent disobedience

Lying, in any form, is not a good idea. That being said, people often describe situations in which lies were used to produce a positive outcome. We must recognize that people may lie to address situations.

> Lying, in any form, is not a good idea.

Suppose a manager has a philosophy that he has applied for many years. He says, "I never tell my team or my senior manager when I am nervous, even if asked. When I have confessed my nervousness, my team doesn't perform to their potential, and my senior manager's reaction and behavior isn't productive."

If someone asks him if he is nervous, this manager will say something like "We have the plans in place to accomplish our goals" or "We will develop plans to accomplish our goal." In this way, nervousness isn't a factor – he believes what he says – but if he *is* nervous, technically, he is lying. He considers the approach to be a small form of intelligent disobedience: he denies truth that would not serve any positive purpose.

This situation is worth scrutiny. Is *any* lie justified under the guise of intelligent disobedience?

This manager's lie passes the "intent test": his lie is not for personal gain, but for the benefit of the business (assuming that his statements about team and senior manager performance are accurate). He is the sole owner of this truth, because nobody but he can leak the truth about his nervousness. Leaking this information, however, is a concern. What if his actions, tone of voice, or focus change in a way that indicates his true emotional state? Although this manager claims success with hiding his nervousness, perhaps trust, unbeknownst to him, has been impacted by his statements. And if that is the case, eroded trust could affect his ability to engage in more substantial acts of intelligent disobedience.

There are higher integrity alternatives to lying. Using a different statement, or silence, may accomplish the same goal. For instance, our nervous manager could have said, "Yeah, I am nervous when running these projects. That's why I focus on putting sound, detailed plans in place." This accomplishes the same outcome, without risking trust. In fact, the honesty of that statement could actually increase trust.

Neither should the power of silence be underestimated. A colleague who was working on a project with tight deadlines was in a meeting with her client, her company's CEO, and her company's sales manager. The client inquired about meeting their aggressive schedule. While the CEO and sales manager boldly promised that the schedule would be met, my colleague remained stoic. After the meeting, the client approached my colleague, confessed that he did not believe the CEO and sales manager, and confidentially asked what she thought would be realistic. Her truth supported the client's intuition, and plans were adjusted to accommodate the pragmatic expectation, preserving business integrity. It also elevated the trust my colleague enjoyed with her client. Two forms of intelligently disobedient silence were utilized in this example: the first was my colleague's silence in the meeting; and the second was the client's self-restraint, not challenging the CEO in the meeting and instead seeking truth afterwards.

> 66 *Is there a difference between lying and not following a closely held business process?* 99

Is there a difference between lying and not following a closely held business process? Both can erode trust when performed in an inappropriate context. The stigma when labelled as a "liar," however, is more damaging and permanent than that of the label "process breaker." "Process breaker" conveys an approach to accomplishing goals. "Liar" is more far-reaching, implying issues with your day-to-day interactions with others.

Be extremely cautious when contemplating a lie. The following are some points to think about.

1   Your lie should follow the same constraints outlined in Chapter 3 for executing intelligent disobedience.
2   Share your lie with the minimum number of people. You may have to double back and correct your false statement.
3   Ensure that lying is the only way of achieving the desired outcome for the business. Examine whether there are truthful ways of conveying information and inspiring appropriate action.
4   Consider a lie only when the truth would be detrimental or would not provide value. Suppose that your business is not delivering the product your client wants, but will in a few days. Telling the client today that the product is available could avert a detrimental outcome, even though it is not truthful at the moment.

   Note: This could backfire if the product's availability date is pushed out.

5   Don't lie as a means of delaying bad news. Bad news ages like milk, not wine. If news is bad and won't change, share the truthful bad news immediately.
6   Prepare for a confrontation about your lie. Be willing to admit lying, and be able to justify your reason for doing so. Be prepared to share the truth and your reasoning as soon as possible.

Is pretending a form of lying?

Authenticity, a significant part of ethical behavior, involves being true to yourself and sharing your views. An example is when you believe an approach won't succeed. What if you decide that your best course of action in a situation is to "go with the flow" and not object to what has been proposed? While you may still hold true to your concerns, your inaction could be construed as pretending that everything is okay.

Pretending could be the worst way of lying if any of the following are true:

- to justify your position, you look only for signs of failure instead of looking for success and promoting actions to improve your organization's chance of positive outcomes;
- you find yourself more concerned about being wrong about your views than wanting the outcomes to be positive;
- you are covertly planning alternative actions rather than surfacing issues about indicators of suboptimal outcomes and focusing on corrections to address them;
- you are aware of others who believe a change to be necessary, but are neglecting to take action because of your current expressed "pretend" position.

If any of these describe your behavior, stop pretending and put your truth on the table. You can do this in the following ways.

- Dedicate your time, or the time of team members, to supporting the success of the current approach.
- Propose interim measures that will demonstrate or forecast the outcomes of the current course of action, whether they are positive or negative. Agree to support the current approach if an acceptable level of positive outcomes is forecast. This establishes the conditions under which you support the current approach.
- Garner support to create alternative plans, draft them openly, and share them. That way, they can be considered if the current activity does not yield the hoped-for outcomes.
- Agree to support the current direction along with the situation(s) that would trigger your alternative plans. Be sure to include specific time frames for assessing metrics to determine whether your alternate plan should be activated.

Engaging in this way promotes a balance between being authentic and supporting your own truth, while also supporting your position within your organization and your perspective regarding current approaches.

Dealing with those who can't handle the truth

Jack Nicholson's portrayal of Colonel Nathan Jessup in the movie *A Few Good Men* is memorable for his quote, "You want the truth? You can't handle the truth!" In the movie, that line triggered a series of events that led to Jessop's downfall. In the real world, disaster doesn't necessarily follow.

Dealing with managers who cannot or will not recognize truths is probably the toughest obstacle to engaging in intelligent disobedience. It takes considerable effort to work with a senior leader who plays ostrich, whether the leader is reluctant to hear bad news, does not have the energy or time to deal with an issue, or has a genuine inability to handle the truth. Persisting in the face of denial can require more courage than any other form of intelligent disobedience.

> 66 *Dealing with managers who cannot or will not recognize truths is probably the toughest obstacle to engaging in intelligent disobedience.* 99

If your persistent support of truth doesn't yield positive results, the following techniques can increase your probability of success with a truth-denying leader.

- *Don't go forward alone.*

  Rarely is it the case that only one person is concerned by their leader's denial of truths. Find others who have experienced the same frustration, and present a united front. If you present information in writing, list the names of all supporters in alphabetical order, to prevent the impression that a ring leader is driving the pack.

  Provide specific detail regarding your concerns about ignoring facts and the outcomes you seek. Use the language of risk and reward. Remove emotion from communication – particularly when your difficult leader reacts emotionally.

  Note: If you alone perceive a problem with your leader's ability to handle truth, it might be your relationship with your leader that needs addressing rather than the inability of the leader to acknowledge truth.

- *Increase your chance of convincing your leader by framing your truths with data from sources your leader trusts.*

  Take note of the leader's decisions and the data used to support them. Compare those with instances in which the leader ignores facts or is indecisive. The comparisons can help you to identify the forms of truth that resonate with your leader. In future situations, gather information of the variety that your leader acts upon, and communicate the origin of that data. (For example, some people prefer data from external sources, while others rely on trusted local advisers.)

- *Do not become frustrated and start ignoring truths yourself.*
  Mirroring a leader's denial of truth is not useful; instead, enhance your truth-collecting tools and approaches.
- *Be persistent and consistent.*
  Never give up. Sometimes, increased truth sharing can win the day with the difficult leader. You may feel like a broken record, but repetition may be exactly what leaders need. Eventually, you may catch them when they are open to your input and ideas, so that they finally "see the truth."

Conclusion

Truth is at the heart of intelligent disobedience. Sharing your truth and inviting others to do the same helps leaders to make informed decisions. In addition, greater quantities of truth from different individuals can set the stage for successful

> 66 *Truth is at the heart of intelligent disobedience.* 99

acts of intelligent disobedience. Remember: no single individual in an organization owns the truth; all individuals in a group own pieces of truth. Collecting and understanding greater breadths of truth increases your leadership capabilities. Sharing truths – often when it is most difficult to do so – can yield the best outcomes. Be diligent and confront people who use your truths in opposition to your intent or objectives.

Bending or breaking rules is commonplace within intelligent disobedience, but lying is to be avoided. However, there are instances in which lying can be successful. Even so, proceed carefully if you decide to employ lying; handled incorrectly, lying can significantly erode trust. Likewise, be careful when you pretend to support something: pretending constitutes a form of lying if not managed properly.

With leaders who will not recognize truths, present a united front, and ensure that you present facts and limit emotion. Recognize the type and source of information to which a difficult leader responds, and use similar truths to present your information more effectively.

Notes

1 Scott, Susan. 2004. *Fierce Conversations: Achieving Success at Work and in Life One Conversation at a Time.* New York: Berkely.
2 Nakashima, Ellen. 2016. Lawmakers say Snowden is in contact with Russian spies but cite no public evidence. *The Washington Post.* [Online]. Available at: https://www.washingtonpost.com/world/national-security/lawmakers-say-snowden-is-in-contact-with-russian-spies-but-cite-no-public-evidence/2016/12/22/591bd074-c886-11e6-bf4b-2c064d32a4bf_story.html?tid=a_inl&utm_term=.cc9ab1ca752d [Accessed 1 May 2017].

Chapter 8

Authorizing control by relinquishing control

Intelligent disobedience is about not only actions you decide to take, but also the latitude you give to others to help to generate business outcomes. Allowing others to engage in intelligent disobedience within defined boundaries expands the quantity and quality of outcomes you can achieve. This chapter explores how to empower your team members, so that they can successfully apply intelligent disobedience to deliver better results.

Characteristics of intelligently disobedient team members

You probably have team members with integrity and the best intentions. However, that isn't enough to apply intelligent disobedience successfully. They might hesitate to act out of fear. Or some actions could feel unnatural to them. Others could struggle with balance, for example consistently supporting clients with no consideration of the cost to your company.

Before you empower team members to engage in intelligent disobedience, you should determine whether they are worthy candidates. To do that, you need to evaluate their behavior, and examine your intuition about them. Considering the following characteristics can aid your evaluation.

Characteristic 1: is driven to contribute

> **❝ *Their jobs are an expression of their vocation* ❞**

People who successfully engage in intelligent disobedience are driven to contribute to the business. They do not take their jobs or their potential impact on the business lightly. Their jobs are an expression of their vocation, not only a way of supporting themselves and their families.

They are equally vocal whether expressing support or concerns regarding a new idea. They often express both when a new idea is shared.

They are aware of their business's measures of success. If measures don't exist or are unclear, they propose their own and how they intend to support them. These contributors collect information about the business, its strategies, changes to the organization chart, new products, and new markets.

They also enjoy learning and driving organizational change. They have fun at work and immerse themselves in the business environment.

Characteristic 2: focuses on short- and long-term business outcomes

Balancing short- and long-term business outcomes is a critical factor for successful intelligent disobedience. Acts of intelligent disobedience need to support the entire business. Benefits to the individual are commonplace and ethical, as long as business outcomes are the highest priority.

Team members should consistently place business outcomes before personal ones before you give them the latitude to engage in intelligent disobedience. When a short-term objective is required, intelligently disobedient individuals focus on those short-term objectives, but they also remain mindful of long-term impacts and what can be done to manage them. They should also be adept at mitigating short-term impacts generated by decisions intended to provide long-range benefits.

Characteristic 3: assesses change ambition

Change ambition is the ability to recognize one's own energy levels compared to those of others. A person's drive to contribute has to be tempered to prevent exhaustion in the rest of the team. For example, an overly driven team member could leave other employees struggling to adopt frequently changing business approaches.

A team member needs to evaluate proposed changes to consider both the big picture of potential outcomes and the details and effort required to implement the change. Your team member should also take into account their own well-being and the well-being of others. A person who works self-imposed long hours and struggles with health and family issues will eventually be absent and not contribute. In addition, other team members will struggle with the expectations of an uncompromising change agent.

Team members who display change ambition develop new processes to facilitate a change, while gauging the organization's appetite and energy to implement the change. They recognize the support needed to ensure that their colleagues understand, appreciate, and can absorb a change. They also know to slow down or postpone a change that overly taxes the organization.

Characteristic 4: displays healthy ownership

Chapter 5 defined healthy ownership as the ability to own what is appropriate and allow others to take responsibility without interfering. People who can apply intelligent disobedience successfully work within their spheres of influence and responsibility, where they have authority to act.

In contrast, people who inappropriately assume responsibility for others, act without advance consultation, or apply intelligent disobedience with righteousness about the inaction of others are not good candidates.

Characteristic 5: builds boundary-based relationships

Constructive, trust-based relationships are a fundamental part of intelligent disobedience, because people must be able to communicate effectively in tense situations. A vital aspect of constructive relationships is appropriate give and take. An individual looking only for praise, who always agrees with others, does not develop relationships with appropriate boundaries. Being totally disagreeable isn't constructive, either. A prerequisite for successful intelligent disobedience is the ability to build relationships in which support and pushback are presented respectfully, with regard for each person's needs and point of view.

Characteristic 6: builds long-term relationships

People who develop relationships only to let them dissolve appear opportunistic and focused on short-term goals. Sincere relationships are lasting, regardless of whether the parties continue to work in the same environment. Long-term relationship builders are adept at establishing new relationships when needed, but also maintain existing contacts.

In long-term relationships, people can offer help or ask for assistance without awkwardness. Support from new and old colleagues is vital to the success of substantial or potentially controversial acts of intelligent disobedience. Longer-term colleagues have the history necessary to share perspectives, contribute to doing the homework that helps to ensure success, and vouch for intent and integrity if concerns arise.

Characteristic 7: is capable of finesse

Influencing senior leaders while engaging in acts of intelligent disobedience may require everything from blunt communication to persuasive subtlety. The path to success may be a tightrope between communicating without sugar coating and guiding senior leaders to draw their own conclusions. This communicational finesse has no formula; it requires the ability to read the audience and sensitivity to someone's frame of mind. The more finesse someone commands, the greater their ability to successfully communicate the intent and objectives of intelligent disobedience.

How and when to check in

Someone who obtains authority to utilize intelligent disobedience does not automatically feel confident or equipped to capitalize on that authority. People who effectively utilize intelligent disobedience have the right mindset: they act with an appropriate amount of independence and communicate the right amount of information. You must test someone's ability and mindset to determine whether you have the right person to engage in intelligent disobedience on your behalf.

The ideal candidate for engaging in intelligent disobedience is willing to listen to the advice and guidance you provide. Then, depending on the situation at hand, they either:

- conduct appropriate homework, confer with you and others as necessary, and then propose a rational approach; or
- engage in intelligently disobedient behavior and brief you as soon as possible.

When delegating authority to someone for the first time, provide advice on successfully applying intelligent disobedience, then monitor their intelligent disobedience actions and provide feedback on their performance. They should grasp what you tell them and apply it in future decision making. As they gain experience with intelligent disobedience, they should show sound judgment without you having to intervene. (Later in this chapter, I explain how to best manage this transition.) On the other hand, team members who lack the necessary confidence will continue to review business conditions and considerations with you before acting.

Consider this example.

A very capable staff member seemed like the ideal candidate to embrace and apply intelligent disobedience. I encouraged him to apply intelligent disobedience and talked through some scenarios. He expressed enthusiasm and confidence about being able to use intelligent disobedience to improve our department's outcomes.

Despite his expressed comfort level, he would falter when it came time to engage in acts of intelligent disobedience, and he would seek reassurance from me or a peer manager. The delays that arose while he tried to reach us diminished the effectiveness of his proposed courses of action. In one case, he initiated an act of intelligent disobedience, and led peers and a client to believe that certain things were going to occur – only to get cold feet and seek permission for what he had already committed to deliver. Our client was disappointed by the delay and what he perceived as conflicting messages, because the staff member's promises had not been fulfilled within appropriate time frames. What should have been a victory for agility in our organization backfired.

We withdrew the authority for this valuable staff member to engage in intelligent disobedience. While he possessed many of the characteristics discussed in this chapter, he did not recognize when to act independently or to get management authority to deliver acts of intelligent disobedience.

Comfort and competence with intelligent disobedience techniques varies

Not everyone can deploy every style of intelligent disobedience. Most people who are successful at intelligent disobedience use only those styles with which they are comfortable and avoid other styles. Approaches that are comfortable for you might feel inappropriate to others. The styles of intelligent disobedience are not only the change approaches of promotion or prevention discussed in Chapter 5. In addition to recognizing someone's inclination toward promotion or prevention, you must also understand your employee's comfort level with different techniques.

> **Most people who are successful at intelligent disobedience use only those styles with which they are comfortable and avoid other styles.**

It's helpful to discuss the expectations for engaging in intelligent disobedience and to understand what your staff members are comfortable (and uncomfortable) with. It's also useful to understand the styles of intelligent disobedience that your team members tend to use or avoid. Try to allow your team members to take legitimate actions that they are comfortable with, even if those actions make you uncomfortable.

Consider the following examples.

- Lorraine is adept at applying intelligent disobedience when she can address business processes without directly challenging people. She is unlikely to challenge a person's decision; instead, she discusses the existing processes and whether the person's decision necessitates altering those processes. Lorraine is happy to work with others on learning opportunities and to allow a person to fail for the sake of long-term learning.

Lorraine's approach isn't the most efficient way of achieving the desired outcome. However, she is comfortable with it, so it is more likely to work for her than trying to challenge people. By authorizing her to act with intelligence disobedience in her own way, you obtain improved outcomes you would not otherwise achieve.

- Kristin, meanwhile, will easily confront and challenge individuals and manage process changes. She is not comfortable allowing something to fail, even slightly. No matter how you may encourage her, she is unlikely to change her behavior around letting things fail. She simply doesn't use that style of intelligent disobedience.

- Dora can confront people and allow failure in the name of learning. She recognizes that wild proposals can test other people's ideas or can generate other legitimate ideas. However, she will not communicate something inaccurate as a means of testing other people's ideas. She cannot tolerate a preposterous idea or statement being attributed to her.

- Sebastian is excellent at managing acts of intelligent disobedience when he knows exactly how he'll address downstream issues. He may promise a client delivery of out-of-stock products, but only if he knows which client he will renegotiate with to shift orders. In contrast, Diana may make a similar promise, even when she doesn't know how she will fulfill the order. She will make the promise and then consider alternatives in production or warehouse storage schemes to deliver. Diana is comfortable with more ambiguity than Sebastian when engaging in intelligent disobedience.

Use scenarios to evaluate candidates for intelligent disobedience

So far, this chapter has focused on identifying those people who are likely to successfully leverage intelligent disobedience and weed out those who are unlikely to be successful. There is no guarantee that someone will act appropriately when using intelligent disobedience. One way of identifying good candidates more accurately is to discuss scenarios in which you believe intelligent disobedience is warranted and others in which it isn't. Evaluating the answers your candidate provides is a valuable means of assessing their suitability and determining boundaries for empowering intelligent disobedience.

Progressive authorization of intelligent disobedience

Intelligent disobedience takes getting used to, even for those inclined to use it. You don't immediately give someone full rein to use any form of intelligent disobedience; instead, you fine-tune the approaches your staff members use over time. After they prove their mastery of each type of flexibility, you can widen their boundaries to engage in intelligent disobedience.

Some people may progress through all of the following levels of authority, while others may stop at a particular type. No matter the progress, the outcome improvement is useful and worth the effort. Each environment is different, so the following types are generic and conceptual. Modify them to suit your business situation.

The four levels of boundary conditions are as follows.

1   Rule benders
2   Rule inventors
3   Rule breakers
4   Actors

Level 1: bending rules or processes

Start someone on their intelligent disobedience journey by allowing them to bend or alter widely held procedures. You can qualify a person's authority by specifying:

- which business processes are within or excluded from their authority to act;
- portions of processes that cannot be bent under any circumstances;
- changes that can be applied without prior authority from management and changes that require a review in advance.

Someone at this level must report to management after using intelligent disobedience to ensure that the results align with expectations.

Level 2: inventing new processes

People who attain this level can still bend rules. They are also permitted to invent new processes in selected process areas – that is, they have the authority to develop and apply new processes in specific process areas and in specific situations, as long as the processes align with the intent and spirit of existing business processes. The result of an invented process should yield the same or improved outcome as the standard process. The new process must be documented, so that it can be repeated if desired.

You can limit a process inventor's boundaries to portions of processes, although inventors normally have more latitude than people at the first level. Usually, inventors can act without reviewing their ideas with management in advance, but they are encouraged to do so if feasible. All outcomes are reviewed with management after implementation, to allow for adjustments and education of the team at large.

Level 3: breaking rules and processes to achieve a desired and defined outcome

Rule breakers have the same boundaries as inventors; the difference is that restrictions to act are the exception, rather than the norm. Rule breakers can overtly break a rule or subvert a process at their discretion. Typically, they can violate process without authorization from managers. However, you can exclude some processes as exceptions that require prior authorization.

Communication to management of the act and outcome of intelligent disobedience is mandatory at this level. Outcomes are typically reviewed in detail only when expected results were not achieved.

Level 4: actors – spontaneous decisions are acceptable

Actors have the same authority to engage in intelligent disobedience as the manager, with rare exceptions. The team member can decide how to communicate, document, and review outcomes, based on their judgment of the manager's needs or expectations defined by the manager.

Mapping intelligent disobedience characteristics to authority levels

In a perfect world, everyone on your team would possess all of the characteristics discussed in this chapter and would attain the level of "actor." Because the world isn't perfect, however, you must consider your employees' characteristics as you identify candidates for intelligent disobedience and help them to progress through levels of authority. Their characteristics should dictate the trust you place in your employees' abilities to engage in various types of intelligent disobedience.

- *All levels of intelligent disobedience require characteristics 1, "is driven to contribute," and 2, "focuses on short- and long-term business outcomes."* Without the drive to contribute, team members won't deliver results consistently and may not perform the required follow-up to intelligently disobedient acts. Because nontraditional approaches affect short-term and long-term outcomes, team members must be attuned to business outcomes. If someone is weak in either of these characteristics, you should plan to provide significant supervision and guidance when you authorize them to act with intelligent disobedience.

- *Inventors must also possess characteristic 3, "assesses change ambition", and 4, "displays healthy ownership."* For new processes to deliver benefits to an organization, a rule inventor must consider the work and stress that a new process can introduce. If the people who use the new process perceive it as overly labor-intensive, they might not follow it, which means that the expected results of the intelligent disobedience will not be realized over the long term.

- *Rule breakers must be able to build strong relationships.* Significant boundary-based relationships (characteristic 5) are required, because rule breakers must do the homework to ensure that their rule breaking is understood and will be effective. Boundary-based relationships also help others to understand that the rule breaking is well intended, especially when the outcome takes time to evolve. With strong long-term relationships (characteristic 6), rule breakers understand the impact to other organizations and can do broader homework when needed.

- *Actors require strength in all seven characteristics.* Spontaneous decisions to act with intelligent disobedience require actors to demonstrate finesse in reading people and situations, as well as to understand the short- and long-term implications of intelligently disobedient acts. Outcomes from intelligent disobedience may never become the norm. For that reason, actors must use finesse to communicate intent and set the expectation that results may not be delivered unless new processes are applied across the business. For example, an actor who makes a spontaneous and significant change to the manufacturing schedule to satisfy the unusual needs of an important client must clearly communicate that changes of that nature are not the norm, because the costs of consistently making those changes would outweigh the benefits.

Table 8.1 is a summary tool outlining the factors, steps, and activity requirements at each level.

An intelligently disobedient interviewing technique: enabling intelligent disobedience with a team

Sometimes, you might allow an entire team to engage in intelligent disobedience. The following is an example of team-based intelligent disobedience that one organization uses to interview prospective employees.

Ken uses a strict rule when interviewing prospective employees: he doesn't spend more than 30 minutes with any candidate whom he doesn't think would come out either first or second on his shortlist. If he spends more than 30 minutes with a candidate, he sees potential, and he will want opinions from his team. Ken's team trusts his assessment of someone's technical skills and background;

Table 8.1 Overview of levels of intelligent disobedience and prerequisite characteristics required for each level

Intelligent disobedience level	Applicable processes	Extent of authority	Intelligent disobedience actions preauthorized?	Review intelligent disobedience action/ results	Document action and results	Minimum characteristics required
Rule benders	Specifically defined by management; portions or processes excluded from intelligent disobedience may be defined as well	May alter existing processes	Only those specifically indicated by management	Always, both approach and results	Always	1,2
Rule inventors	Specifically defined by management; typically, entire process can be altered or bypassed, although, in rare cases, portions of a process can be excluded	May alter existing processes or create new processes	Only those specifically indicated by management	Always, both approach and results	Always	1,2,3,4

(continued)

Table 8.1 (continued)

Intelligent disobedience level	Applicable processes	Extent of authority	Intelligent disobedience actions preauthorized?	Review intelligent disobedience action/ results	Document action and results	Minimum characteristics required
Rule breakers	Specifically defined by management; typically, entire process can be altered or bypassed, although, in rare cases, portions of a process can be excluded	May alter existing processes, create new processes, or break the rules of existing processes	Typically, no, but some processes may need preauthorization	Acts and outcomes are communicated; they are reviewed only when results were not as intended	Typically, yes, but some exceptions are allowed for more unusual acts that will probably not be repeated	1,2,3,4,5,6
Actors	Authority typically matches that of the manager	Has full authority to alter existing, create new, or break rules	Typically, no, but on rare occasion a process may need preauthorization	Communication and review at discretion of the actor, unless outcome was not as intended, then a review occurs	At the discretion of the actor	All seven

Characteristics: 1 – driven to contribute; 2 – focuses on short- and long-term business outcomes; 3 – assesses change ambition; 4 – displays healthy ownership; 5 – builds boundary-based relationships; 6 – builds long-term relationships; 7 – is capable of finesse however, it is important to the entire group that any candidate's personality fit with the team.

Ken and his team use a clever method for quickly and accurately assessing a job candidate's character. The team knows to initiate this method when Ken spends more than 30 minutes with a candidate. They convene in the breakroom and set up two games of Jenga, a block-stacking game in which players try to remove blocks without toppling the stack. One Jenga game is set up at the table with the more introverted team members. The more boisterous extroverts on the team play the game at another table.

After Ken's interview, he brings the candidate to the breakroom and introduces the team. The team extends a welcome, along with an invitation to join either of the Jenga games. Ken and his team use this approach to assess the candidate's:

- ability to deal with unexpected situations;
- comfort level dealing with extroverts and introverts;
- sense of humor (the team members joke with each other as they play);
- desire to fit in and learn about the team members (the team asks the candidate questions and share information about themselves);
- competitive nature, based on how seriously the candidate takes winning the Jenga game;
- ability to laugh at themselves (the team teases the candidate if they feel comfortable).

Over several years and numerous staff additions, Ken and his team have had very few surprises with candidates hired using the "Jenga test."

Conclusion

You can increase the quantity and quality of beneficial outcomes to your business by providing mindful opportunities for your staff to engage in intelligent disobedience. Before you give someone authority to initiate acts of intelligent disobedience, you need to evaluate their suitability and then decide the level of intelligent disobedience at which you expect them to perform. You can also question candidates about how they would act in various scenarios, as a final test.

You need to plan a team member's growth into higher levels of intelligent disobedience, and nurture it with encouragement and guidance. As someone successfully navigates lower levels, you can authorize increasingly substantial acts of intelligent disobedience. Although this effort isn't trivial, it can improve your organization's business outcomes and enhance your career.

Note: The stories throughout this book were the result of intelligently disobedient actions taken by someone empowered to act with intelligent disobedience (either overtly by a manager or self-directed and communicated after the event). This empowerment was not provided for a single instance of intelligent disobedience; individuals typically progress through levels of more sophisticated actions, based on the abilities they display.

Chapter 9

Storytelling

Storytelling is not an act of intelligent disobedience. However, earning support for acts of intelligent disobedience or conveying the reason for them calls for well-crafted communication. Stories are a great way to communicate that infor-

❝ *Stories are a great way to communicate* ❞

mation. Business leaders around the world are learning how powerful stories can be in the workplace.

More than just a communication of facts, effective storytelling leaves a lasting impression. Stories can change our attitudes, beliefs, and behaviors. A *Harvard Business Review* article recommends that business people begin every presentation with a compelling, human-scale story.[1] To be effective, stories must be at the appropriate level of detail and presented at the right time.

Enhancing stories with effective tools will help you to succeed with intelligent disobedience. This chapter provides tips and hints for developing and conveying effective stories. It also highlights tools that you can use with those stories – particularly when talking with busy senior leaders.

The 30-second/3-minute/30-minute approach

Stories are more powerful when shared in the right context and at the right time. Getting the attention of a senior leader for any reason is challenging, but it's crucial when you want to justify or explain an act of intelligent disobedience. Many leaders, in their enthusiasm, ambush their senior leader and try to tell the entire story they've worked hard to perfect. While that may work if you catch a busy manager at a quiet time, it's not recommended. A more effective approach is the "30/3/30" approach, which packs the story into short pieces (30 seconds, 3 minutes) to get your senior leader's attention. Then, when the time is right, you can tell the whole story (30 minutes).

With this approach, you create three versions of your story. You begin by crafting the full 30-minute story, with all of the detail you want to convey. Then, you pare that down into a 3-minute story. Finally, you distill that into a 30-second story with which you'll get your leader's attention.

The following sections describe how each of these stories is used.

The 30 seconds

A 30-second summary explains why you need time with your busy senior leader. With this brief summary, you can convey urgency in a brief hallway conversation, a short email, or a message that an executive assistant can share with their boss. An effective summary compels your senior leader to make time for further conversation – or perhaps to continue the hallway conversation you're having. That's where the 3-minute story comes into play.

The 3 minutes

Once your 30-second pitch gets your leader's attention, it's time to share a slightly more detailed version of your story. This 3-minute version should cover the most significant details, explaining why you or your senior leader should engage in intelligent disobedience to achieve better outcomes. If the leader isn't interested in continuing, this could be the end of your storytelling effort. If more discussion is required, you can request a 30-minute meeting.

The 30 minutes

The goal of the 30-minute meeting is a decision about whether and how to act with intelligent disobedience. You share the full details of your story, adding in details you left out of the 30-second and 3-minute versions. Ideally, your entire story should be no more than 8–10 minutes long. After finishing your story, use the rest of the 30 minutes to discuss the nature of your intended outcomes and why current processes, practices, or expectations will yield suboptimal results. Share your truth, and invite others to put truths on the table, so that a sound decision can be made.

"Gold rings" or "aspirin"

The story you share via the 30/3/30 model must be relevant to the senior leader you address. To use the 30/3/30 approach effectively, the crux of the story needs to be clear and meaningful, to break through the clutter of items crossing your leader's desk. To get action, your stories need to highlight a "gold ring" – a significant step forward or improvement in outcomes – or "aspirin" – something that relieves pain or a shortcoming. Without one or both of those, your story is likely to be filed or deleted.

Note: It's challenging to make your story stand out from the many relevant items the leader hears every day. Leadership is often full of burdens and flash decisions. At one point in my career, I received more than 250 emails every day. I could easily spend every workday just reading emails. Add meeting requests, briefings for customers, and briefings for the boss, and I would be overloaded from dawn till dusk. The biggest challenge is making many flash decisions accurately – because deciding what to act on, delegate, file or delete is difficult.

> " *To get action, your stories need to highlight a "gold ring" - a significant step forward or improvement in outcomes - or "aspirin" - something that relieves pain or a shortcoming.* "

A 30/3/30 story example

The following is a case study, along with the three versions of the story used to convince the chief information officer (CIO) to take action.

Updating PC software in a colleague's insurance company is an increasingly difficult and expensive endeavor. Individual departments add software to their desktops without a screening process. Employees add their own analysis software to streamline their jobs. While these customizations help employees, they create a nightmare for the support team who maintain desktop computers. There are concerns with data security, virus protection, and collaboration capabilities. Data security is of particular concern, because updates from Microsoft and virus-protection vendors need to be applied to the computers quickly and efficiently. Although no data security or virus issues have yet occurred, the risks are increasing.

30-second version

I'd like to discuss the increasing risk of data security and virus breaches in our environment. The effort and cost of maintaining the desktops and applying new software has almost doubled in recent months. Without intervention, costs and risk will continue to rise.

Note: This summary points out pain that the CIO might not have been aware of and implies that "aspirin" is available.

Additions to create the 3-minute story

- Add that there is little control of the desktop environment. Employees add software to their PCs without evaluation by the CIO's team.
- Present the cost and time required to implement software updates across all desktops, which has been analyzed and quantified.
- Confirm that the business is exposed to cyberattacks because of the delays in adding virus control and data security updates.
- Present the nature of the intervention or solution: restricting the employees' ability to load software onto their PCs themselves and restricting the PCs to a standard set of configurations, called standard operating environments (SOEs).

30-minute meeting content

- Present the nature of the problem, propose a solution, and clarify the meeting objectives.
- Present and discuss the broad software inventory in use across PCs in the current environment.
- Explain that employees have positive intent by using self-loaded software to increase productivity. However, to prevent negative business impact, desktops running various software combinations are being tested extensively, which takes a long time, at significant cost.
- Discuss software packages that can be consolidated or eliminated.
- Propose a limited set of SOEs: one for general PC users, and others to address the needs of the business where specialty or highly technical software packages are required
- Review a schedule for performing the work to create the SOEs.
- Highlight how to handle communication to employees, along with how to manage implementation of the SOEs.

Utilizing tools: information-rich, single-page diagrams

Presenting stories with a well-designed single-page graphic is a great way of supporting the 30/3/30 concept. Dan Roam has written a useful book on this topic, called *Back of the Napkin*.[2] His recommendations include pictures that solve the "who/what," "how much," "where," "when," "how," and "why" problems that exist. In addition, he has pragmatic recommendations for how to use diagrams to sell ideas.

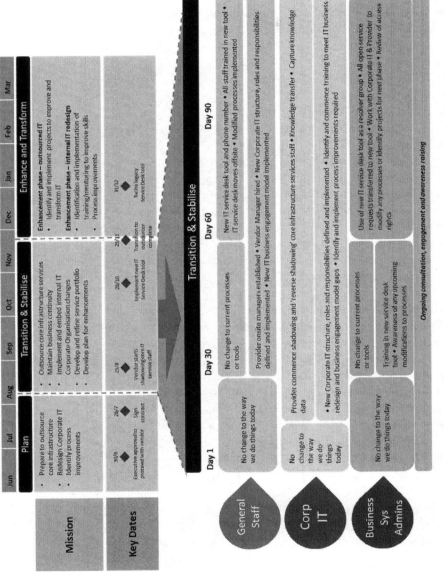

Figure 9.1 Example of a one-page informational diagram showing the plan for a change initiative and the business areas in which change impacts will occur

Many of the pictures discussed in Roam's book, along with common diagrams such as timelines, can be enhanced with focused information and used in 30/3/30 discussions. Figure 9.1 is an example of a one-page diagram that conveys various aspects of a change initiative. It includes the overall objectives, a timeline, a description of the phase life cycle, details of the current phase, and an organizational change management view, all on a single sheet of paper. It is information-rich, but not so busy that you cannot find useful information.

Many discussions could be initiated from this one-page diagram, including:

- the overall status of the initiative;
- when key stakeholders need to be involved and what they need to do;
- upcoming key dates;
- when various parts of the organization need to be prepared to support changes.

In addition, a few marks with a highlighter could emphasize other issues to convey in a 30-second pitch. For example, you might demonstrate the impacts to benefits realization if decisions are not made in a timely fashion. This is demonstrated in Figure 9.2.

Figure 9.3 is a quick reference card that was provided to customers who contact the organization's helpdesk. It describes the options that clients can use to request the service.

This initial draft card was useful before it was deployed to the users of the helpdesk service, because it highlighted the options available, including the large number of options available via online self-service. However, one review and a 30-second conversation simplified it to the new quick reference card shown in Figure 9.4.

In addition to demonstrating complexity, a one-page view can be used to:

- prevent confusion for users by outlining the implications if new steps are added to the support process (Figure 9.5);
- show the positive effects of simplified menu changes to the "portal access approach" to obtain services (Figure 9.6).

One-page diagrams can also outline the steps required to bring a change initiative to fruition. This includes highlighting the impacts to stakeholders and providing high-level timeline information. The one-page diagram in Figure 9.7 shows future scenarios for travelers, including applying for a visa, flying overseas, and clearing customs in a different country. This represents a possible "customer journey" improvement in a concise, understandable format.

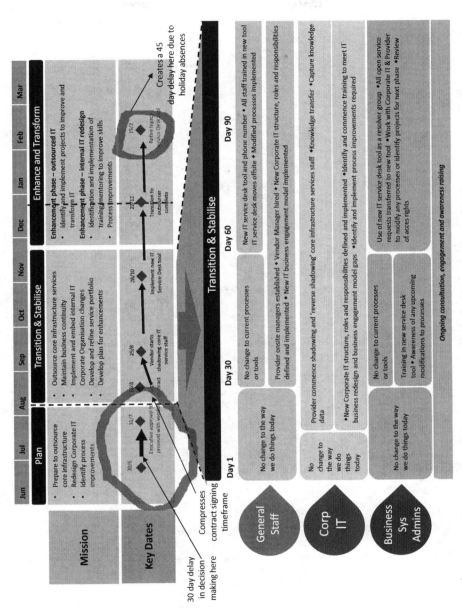

Figure 9.2 Example of quickly altering a one-page informational diagram to tell a different story

24/7 IT Service Desk
Quick Reference Guide

If its URGENT ... **MAKE A PHONE CALL**	**1-800 111-1111 (x1111)**

If its less urgent, you can choose from 3 ways to access the Service Desk ...

☎ **1-800 111-1111 (x1212)**

www **servicedesk@site.com**

🖥 Click "service desk" on the Intranet to access self service portal

If you choose to EMAIL ...

Include a summary in the subject line, and more detail in the body of the email

If you choose to use the self service portal...

Step 1: Click Service Desk on the intranet or go to www.XXXXXXXXXXXXXXXX (no passwords needed as the tool knows who you are based on your computer login)

Step 2: You will be presented with the homepage depicted below. From here, using the <u>menu on the left</u> or the <u>icons on the page</u>, you can:

Step 3: If you are making a request which requires approval, you will need to complete an approval form, which you can find at XXXXXXXXXXXXXX

Step 4: Once fulfilled or resolved, your approval to close the 'ticket' will be requested via email.

A detailed User Guide is available on the intranet at guidespot.place

Figure 9.3 Example of a one-page quick reference guide for use in a service helpdesk

24/7 IT Service Desk
Quick Reference Guide

1-800 111-1111 (x1212)
Use extension 1111 if urgent

Email: servicedesk@site.com

Include a summary in the subject line, and more detail in the body of the email

Intranet

Step 1: Click Service Desk on the intranet or go to www.serviceportal.place

Step 2: You will be presented with the homepage depicted below. From here, using the <u>menu on the left</u> or the <u>icons on the page</u>, you can:

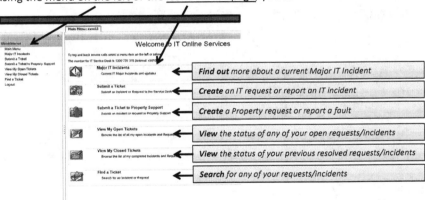

Step 3: If you are making a request which requires approval, you will need to complete an approval form, which you can find at approvalspot.place

A detailed User Guide is available on the intranet at guidespot.place

Figure 9.4 Simplified version of the quick reference guide for a service helpdesk

24/7 IT Service Desk
Quick Reference Guide

1-800 111-1111 (x1212)
Use extension 1111 if urgent

Email: servicedesk@site.com

Include a summary in the subject line, and more detail in the body of the email

Intranet

Step 1: Click Service Desk on the intranet or go to www.serviceportal.place

Step 2: You will be presented with the homepage depicted below. From here, using the <u>menu on the left</u> or the <u>icons on the page</u>, you can:

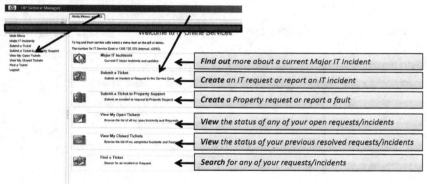

Step 3: If you are making a request which requires approval, you will need to complete an approval form, which you can find at approvalspot.place

Step 4/5: If your request is accepted, you need to notify the service desk when you want the request to be satisfied by going to implementspot.place. If rejected, you need to resubmit the request or withdraw it via the self service portal.

A detailed User Guide is available on the intranet at guidespot.place

Figure 9.5 Example demonstrating how adding new steps to a reference guide can create confusion for clients (see step 4/5 at the bottom of the page)

24/7 IT Service Desk
Quick Reference Guide

1-800 111-1111 (x1212)
Use extension 1111 if urgent

Email: servicedesk@site.com

Include a summary in the subject line, and more detail in the body of the email

Intranet

Step 1: Click Service Desk on the intranet or go to www.serviceportal.place

Step 2: You will be presented with the homepage depicted below. From here, using the <u>menu on the left</u> or the <u>icons on the page</u>, you can:

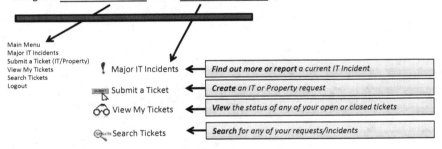

Step 3: If you are making a request which requires approval, you will need to complete an approval form, which you can find at approvalspot.place

A detailed User Guide is available on the intranet at guidespot.place

Figure 9.6 Example of how a simplified menu approach can make selecting a service option much easier for clients

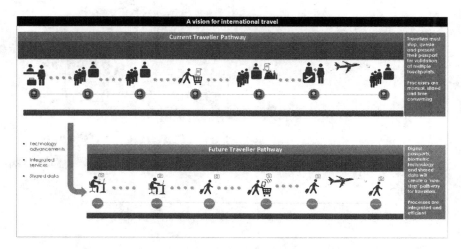

Figure 9.7 One-page diagram to describe a potential change to a customer experience

This diagram could also be used to highlight changes in a 30-second conversation, for instance demonstrating the impacts of additional traveler volumes on screening timing (Figure 9.8).

Alternatively, you can also demonstrate the impacts of additional screening requirements (Figure 9.9).

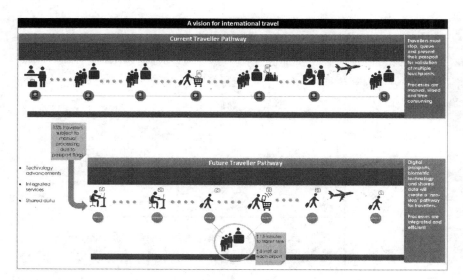

Figure 9.8 One-page diagram to describe the effects of an increase in traveler volume

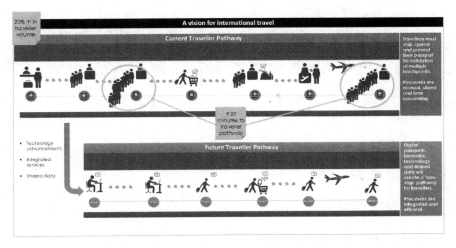

Figure 9.9 One-page diagram to describe a potential change to the traveler experience and airport personnel

Familiar dialog and scenarios

To ensure that your stories are fully understood, use language and scenarios familiar to the listener. You can learn about your audience by reading company reports, listening to senior leaders' use of terminology, and understanding statements of objectives for your organization. Incorporating this information into your stories is powerful way of engaging your listeners.

The use of props is another effective approach. One team struggling with a lack of decision making at a hospital used a prop to support their well-crafted story and compelled their management team to proceed with a needed improvement. The community hospital team was struggling with an old and antiquated patient discharge process. The discharge process had become awkward as a result of process changes made elsewhere in the hospital, law changes, and insurance process alterations. Funding to improve the process was allocated, then repeatedly distributed to other areas deemed more important. While those decisions were logical at the time, the prolonged inaction on patient discharge changes was introducing patient care risks, including prescription errors and overlooked appointment scheduling with specialists. These errors could spell real trouble for a patient requiring further care after discharge.

Rather than repeat the presentation style used in the past, the patient discharge team decided to change their approach. Embracing both intelligent disobedience and storytelling, the leader of the team shared "a patient's tale" with the board.

The story described a seriously ill patient whose life was saved by the diligent efforts of the hospital staff, only for the patient to become ill again after leaving the hospital because of an error in his discharge record. As the presenter neared the conclusion, members of his team rolled in a crash cart – that is, a table with a heart monitor and defibrillation machine. The heart monitor was turned on, and a bright green flat line moved across the screen, accompanied by the monotone sound of a stopped heart. Shock spread across the room, as the board attendees expected to hear that the patient had died from the discharge inaccuracy. The team leader concluded by saying that the patient was fine: it was a fictional story, but only because a final, manual review of the patient's discharge record caught a prescription error. The crash cart was appropriate, continued the team leader, because the current discharge process was dead on arrival. The board approved the funds to update the patient discharge record process – and, this time, the improvements were implemented.

The language of risk and reward: triggering emotions

A story that triggers emotion can energize the listener. Rewards (more substantial outcomes to be achieved), avoidance of risk, or both should be at the heart of your business stories. Fact-based tales that lead your listeners to anticipate an outcome are an effective way in which to inspire action.

The hospital crash cart story was told as if it were factual, except for the patient becoming sick after discharge. The emotion came from the audience presuming the conclusion of the story. The discharge team told stories in a business scenario using the language of risk or reward – framed in facts. The crash cart reinforced their message.

The language of risk and reward is an expansion of the "gold ring" or "aspirin" analogy. The gold ring is conveyed by describing rewarding outcomes; in contrast, risks describe the negative consequences that could occur if a change is not made. The following sections provide some examples.

The reward: changing ideas about training

Management wanted to improve the throughput of their sales staff. A training program was initiated to increase sales productivity. After a few months, the sales staff gave positive feedback regarding the training program, but throughput and revenue did not increase. When challenged, the sales staff shared issues with juggling administrative tasks, which impeded their ability to deploy the training tips and generate more sales. It turned out that the training was misaligned: it focused on building sales skills, when the issue was administrative, relating to process efficiency. The true problem and subsequent reward from alleviating the problem needed to be communicated to management.

The reward statement to management that changed the training direction was:

> Employee skills are not the problem; our approach to solving the issue is the problem. We can reap the reward of increased revenue if we a) share the time-management strategies our best-performing sales people use to get through the day, and b) work on more efficient processing of orders to reduce the burden on the sales team. We will initially experience a negative impact when we take our best sales staff members off the road to discuss and document their time-management habits. We also need to postpone initiatives to redesign other administrative processes. However, if those two impacts cost us $100,000, a 2% sales-productivity increase will recover that upfront cost in only 4 months. The ongoing reward far outweighs the short-term impacts.

The risk: understanding the cost of not spending money

An elevator installation and maintenance company prided itself on old-school values and personal service. Its reputation in the market was solid. Being "old school" served the company well. However, its old-school approach extended to its back-office support processes, including the tracking of onsite service for the equipment the company contracted to maintain. Its systems were homegrown and 26 years old. Its IT team were struggling to keep them up and running. When a mandatory security update was released by Microsoft, the IT staff had to install four other software packages just to keep the company's software running. To make matters worse, the additional software decreased response time. Management, fearing the impact of a significant change with their long-term staff members and the cost of a major system change, was indecisive about replacing the old systems.

A significant statement of risk served as a catalyst for the organization to upgrade its systems:

> The recent mandatory security upgrade cost $75,000 in staff time and will cost an additional $18,000 for software licenses each year. Those costs could increase with the next mandatory upgrade. The estimated cost to replace our old system is $1.8 million. If the current system fails, which is increasingly likely, we run the risk of not performing vital elevator maintenance. People could get hurt or killed. The average settlement of a lawsuit resulting from an elevator accident is $220,000 per person impacted. Most accidents impact multiple individuals. The cost of inaction and reduction of trust from the marketplace are great.

Intelligent disobedience and the business case

Sometimes, the stories we need to share aren't as short as the previous reward and risk examples. At times, they need to be extensive and formal, such as a business case for a large initiative.

Similar to the elevator maintenance company story, the managers of the plumbing products division of a national hardware equipment company were convinced they had to upgrade their warehouses, distribution processes, and shipping vendors to offset the risks posed by agile, Internet-based competitors. The benefits were significant, but costly. Further complicating the business case justification was a corporate mandate that any initiative that cost more than US$1 million had to provide a 15 percent or greater return on investment (ROI) within three years. The improvements being considered were intended to retain market share, rather than to improve it, so the ROI target presented an issue, as well as an opportunity to consider engaging in intelligent disobedience.

The management team pushed back on the 15 percent ROI mandate, stating that continuing with their current distribution processes was too risky: customers were apt to go elsewhere, and the resulting impact to revenue and market reputation was substantial. They admitted that the impact was hard to quantify. The corporate board did not accept this argument. They said that a new system provided an opportunity to closely examine and refine the company's distribution processes, leading to increased efficiency and reduced costs. The 15 percent ROI would have to be demonstrated and committed to before they would authorize replacing their warehousing and distribution model.

The plumbing managers decided that further discussion of this situation was inappropriate: not only would it decrease the probability of the business case being approved, but also further debates at periodic board meetings would take too long.

Faced with the risk of short-term reduction in market share, the team faced a dilemma: how to write a business case for a logistics model with vendors who weren't selected or contracted, and determine a set of savings objectives that were feasible, as well as achievable, for warehouse and logistics line and middle managers.

This dilemma presented a significant requirement for good storytelling, as well as a test of boundaries for intelligent disobedience. A tale that was too encouraging could lead to issues if the actual achievement were to fall short. But being too conservative relative to the 15 percent ROI target would mean no authority to spend the money, putting the business at risk.

The intent here is not to provide a primer on good business case writing, but to emphasize the need to define guidelines for intelligent disobedience in the context of describing future business benefits. While your situation may call for other credibility tests, successfully embracing intelligent disobedience in this context means that you should undertake the following.

- Consult with the affected managers, no matter how hard that may be. Choosing an intelligently disobedient improvement target for others, without reviewing the reward and risk balance, simply postpones significant and potentially indefensible protests from those people or groups.
- Review the history of the organization's ability to absorb and deploy change. If no initiative has yielded greater than 5 percent improvement, it's foolish to commit to a significantly better result without a well-defined tool or process change to achieve it.
- Analyze the timing of the last process or tool change that affected each business area. With the speed of improvements in tools and technology, process improvements every two to three years is feasible. If productivity improvements or changes were made more recently, each area should be examined closely to determine whether existing tools and processes can be used more effectively, rather than opting for another change to technology or deploying entirely new business processes.
- Apply caution with improvements based on time savings. A productivity improvement that is forecast to yield 5 hours per week per person is favorable, but only if those saved hours are put to good use elsewhere. Saved time does not add money to your bank account unless it is for something like hourly contract staff, who can be dismissed.
- Use industry association data, when available. You could be the industry leader, but it is wise to determine whether you are projecting efficiencies or cost reductions that are significantly different from the norm, especially if you don't know how you will accomplish the feat.

With a business case or other forecast, it is best to determine the boundaries surrounding what is reasonable before taking action. If intelligent disobedience is required, be sure to consult with others, and limit your actions to practical feasibility.

Helping others to craft their own stories

The most powerful stories can be those you help other people to craft for themselves. Those stories help your colleagues to gain confidence that a business direction is sound.

A client of mine was struggling with a large change initiative. He was asked to lead an integration of business practices for four

The most powerful stories can be those you help other people to craft for themselves.

different businesses that had been merged into a single organization. The initiative was challenging, because existing business processes were significantly different, and the management team was geographically dispersed. Not all parties were pleased with the merger, so dedication to the task was a risk.

During a conversation, he posed the question, "Do you think we are going to get a result from this that will help the business?" While tempted to answer that question directly, it was more important that my client believed in his ability to get the outcome he wanted. I turned the question back to him, with my own suggestion: "Let's take an inventory of the things you've done thus far to get the outcome you want."

Before long, he had compiled a comprehensive list, including putting together a detailed plan, engaging with both enthusiastic and skeptical people to get them on board, compiling a cost forecast and revising it after discoveries were made, multiple check-in meetings with the CEO to ensure that he supported the approaches, compiling a detailed risk plan and communicating it to key stakeholders, and reviewing plans from other merger initiatives. We brainstormed the issues that plagued other merger efforts. Those issues were all addressed by the activities listed or the risk plan, which included mitigation actions. We then reconsidered the question: did he think he was going to get the results that would help the business? His smile gave me the answer: he had the story he could share with his key stakeholders.

Conclusion

Storytelling is a powerful tool that helps to justify intelligent disobedience. Determining the story to tell and having different-length versions of your story helps you to get the attention of busy senior leaders and to ensure that they understand what you need to convey. Using well-crafted pictures as tools to complement your story is effective. They can be modified easily to represent outcomes that you're trying to achieve or avoid. It's also powerful to help others to craft their own stories. This effort helps to convince them of the validity or folly of the direction they're considering, as well as helps them to share their proposed directions with other managers.

Notes

1 Zak, Paul J. 2014. Why your brain loves good storytelling. *Harvard Business Review* [Online]. Available at: https://hbr.org/2014/10/why-your-brain-loves-good-storytelling [Accessed 17 May 2017].
2 Roam, Dan. 2009. *Back of the Napkin: Solving Problems and Selling Ideas with Pictures*. New York: Portfolio.

Chapter 10

Lessons learned

Intelligent disobedience requires conviction for improving outcomes, clear thinking, courage, and the patience to consider options. This chapter presents lessons learned from intelligent disobedience that failed because those characteristics were out of alignment. The examples in this chapter aren't complete failures, though: the leaders learned from these experiences and continued being disobedient, but in more intelligent ways. These stories help you to consider obstacles that can surface if you do not appropriately prepare to execute intelligent disobedience.

Overestimating the depth of a relationship

Josh is a sales representative with a great reputation. He is especially adept at repairing broken relationships: he frequently works with clients who have become dissatisfied. Josh embraces intelligent disobedience to bring products and services to his clients, and to restore their trust. To support his relationships, he purposefully carves out time to review his interactions with his former, current, and potential clients, as well as contacts inside his company. People like Josh and assist him when they can, knowing that he will return the favor.

Josh was asked to call on a client whose chief financial officer had been replaced with Norman, with whom Josh had worked before. He felt confident in their relationship, which he had maintained with a short conversation six weeks earlier. He felt very comfortable with Norman – even knowing where Norman lived.

Josh was juggling his priorities, and was having difficulty finding a time when he and Norman could meet. He was anxious to touch base with Norman and to determine how he could support him, given Norman's expanded responsibilities. Josh was passing through Norman's town and decided it was time for a small bit of intelligent disobedience. Knowing that Norman was an early riser, Josh showed up at Norman's house at 7.30 am to invite him to breakfast. Norman was not happy to see Josh at his door; he dismissed him with a firm direction not to schedule time on his calendar.

Fortunately for Josh, Norman reached out a couple of weeks later. Norman opened the meeting by explaining that his trust in Josh had been diminished. He said that someone so anxious to have a discussion is "trying too hard" and was not to be trusted. Because of their prior relationship, however, Norman forgave Josh and continued to work with him.

Josh learned two lessons from this.

- He'd had too much confidence in his relationship with Norman. While his history with Norman saved the day, Josh had never been invited to Norman's house for any reason. Josh had overstepped Norman's boundaries.
- Josh's intelligent disobedience impacted on someone other than himself without prior discussion. Josh was accommodating his own calendar need and did not consider the impact on Norman. Any intelligent disobedience that has an impact on others needs to be reviewed in advance.

A lack of homework and communication

Kathie is the logistics planning manager for a large printing company. She supports the distribution of paper, binding supplies, and other materials to her company's facilities. She also coordinates the assignment of print jobs to 16 facilities and distribution of final products to clients. It's a fast-paced role, with quickly changing client demands, equipment issues, and distribution problems to resolve. Kathie frequently shifts print jobs from one facility to another or spreads large jobs over multiple facilities to accommodate client needs and manage delivery constraints. She will also push facility limits, asking staff members to produce above their standard capacity, or will deploy extra drivers and book air cargo to distribute their product when client benefits justify the additional cost.

Kathie succeeds at pushing the limits because she understands the facility's actual versus published capacities, based on detailed knowledge of the equipment in each location. She also knows which staff members are willing to go the extra mile. Keeping this knowledge current takes considerable time: staff turnover and equipment updates frequently change the capabilities of each site.

At one point, flu hit a large percentage of drivers at a print facility, creating a hectic time for Kathie. She quickly shifted work to another facility, but did not verify whether they could handle 120 percent of normal workload. She felt confident, however, because a few days earlier she had noted that the facility had a reasonable job queue and good staff availability. After making the job transfer, she went home for the evening.

The next morning, her cellphone did not stop ringing. Panicked calls and texts let Kathie know that her shift of work had gone very wrong. Two print machines were being serviced at the facility to which she had moved the work. There was no way the job would be completed on time. Her new manager heard about the issue before Kathie did, creating a trust issue.

The first lesson that Kathie learned was fundamental: she neglected to do her homework to identify the current limitations of the facility. However, her problem was magnified because she hadn't told her manager that she shifts jobs among sites, sometimes exceeding their published capacity. Although her tactic had not caused a problem prior to this incident, the lack of communication irked her new manager.

An intended outcome, but the wrong result

Lee is a manager who advocates fairness in his job at a global technology company. This fairness was tested when he accepted Marvin's transfer into his department. Marvin had moved back to where he grew up to be closer to his family. Although new to the department, he jumped in and immediately contributed. He was jovial, worked well with his teammates and the client, and was always willing to lend a hand and share ideas. Lee was pleased to have him on the team.

After a month, Marvin told Lee that he was concerned about his salary. Lee agreed with Marvin's concern. He had reviewed his team's salaries a few days earlier and determined that Marvin was being underpaid. Lee said that he would investigate alternatives to make salary adjustments. He did not make any promises, since he would have to work any adjustments through the company's considerable bureaucracy.

Lee pursued the salary adjustments and updated Marvin periodically. Even though Marvin said he understood, Lee could sense that Marvin was growing impatient. Marvin's contribution to the department did not diminish, so Lee decided not to worry.

Eventually, Lee thought of an intelligently disobedient approach. He had access to performance bonuses and an annual salary increase allocation. He shared his plan with Marvin: he allocated bonus dollars to Marvin and discussed a set of performance objectives that would allow Marvin to collect a second bonus in three months. It was highly unusual for bonuses to be given this close together. Lee also implemented the highest salary increase allowed. Finally, he would submit Marvin for a formal salary review six months after the second bonus. Marvin expressed appreciation for the effort and additional money – but Lee's intuition was triggered: Marvin's appreciation didn't seem heartfelt.

As the time approached for Marvin's second bonus, a few teammates commented about Marvin aggressively pushing himself and the team. They were informal comments made in passing, so Lee did not take action.

Marvin satisfied the criteria for his second bonus, which he accepted with a sincere "thank you." He also pressed Lee to immediately perform a salary review. Lee assured Marvin that he was already pushing the salary management standards. A request for an earlier review would be rejected and decrease Marvin's chance for a salary adjustment.

For the next six months, Marvin continued to deliver for the department. Lee kept his promise and requested a salary review for Marvin. Unfortunately, Lee's manager, who was a stickler for following process, was out of the office with an extended illness. Lee decided that he could share the salary increase and outcome with his manager upon his return. The salary review yielded a 3 percent increase for Marvin – less than Lee had hoped. Considering the unusual approach, however, he was pleased to get something for Marvin.

Marvin thought the 3 percent wasn't enough. Lee explained again that he was going out on a limb for Marvin. However, within a month, Marvin applied for a family hardship transfer request to another office to move to a climate better suited for an ill family member.

Lee hesitated, considering Martin's salary pressure and his short time in the department. Marvin appealed to HR and was granted a transfer.

Lee later found out that the family move was not for health reasons. Marvin resigned after only six months in his new department. Lee confirmed that Marvin appealed salary decisions made by his new manager before leaving the company.

Lee shared the following reflections.

- He should have acted on his intuition and talked with Marvin to assess Marvin's true feeling about his salary and to try to adjust Marvin's perception of his salary package.
- Lee felt that Marvin's salary adjustment was fair, which was a good outcome.
- Despite the good outcome, the result was not satisfactory to Lee: he lost an employee in his group and, ultimately, the company. He had misread Marvin, ignoring some danger signs. Marvin was out for himself, with little regard for loyalty, even when Lee stuck his neck out for him. Lee should have used the salary and bonus allocations on other loyal, well-performing members of his team.
- Lee did not brief his manager appropriately. His manager was not pleased with Lee's initiating a second salary review. Although not technically in violation of the rules, the salary review, combined with two bonus payments, was not deemed acceptable. Lee lost the ability to be flexible with future salary allocations.

- Lee felt strongly about being fair, as well as having a degree of autonomy in performing his job. Part of ignoring his intuition, Lee admits, could have come from a desire to do things his way, even while knowing his manager would probably be displeased. But personal rebellion should never be a reason for engaging in intelligent disobedience.

> *personal rebellion should never be a reason for engaging in intelligent disobedience.*

After working with Marvin, Lee adjusted his approach to intelligent disobedience. He now spends more time looking at future considerations before he acts, to make sure that the short- and long-term results are both positive.

Unhealthy ownership: intelligent disobedience becomes expected

Tanya was thrilled when she landed a senior sales representative job with a major software company. This was her first senior role with her own clients and the autonomy to manage them her way. She was building her sales portfolio according to plan when one of her key technical architects got sick and a second went on maternity leave. Concerned that newer technical team members would not appropriately support her clients, she feared that her promises for delivering business outcomes would fall short. The intelligently disobedient solution was obvious to her: she still trusted her own technical capabilities, so she would become a "ghost architect" until she could resolve her technical resource issue.

Initially, Tanya's approach worked extremely well. Adding the technical work actually helped her: she learned more about her clients and their needs. To prevent the client from thinking that the team was short of quality resources, however, she performed her architecture work outside their offices. And concerned that her new management would think she was unable to delegate well, she kept her dual role to herself.

The hours soon became taxing. And, to make matters worse, her ill architect had to extend his sick leave.

During her next quarterly review, Tanya received a glowing report. The highlight of the review was her manager saying that she was the best at utilizing technical team members. "I'm totally impressed," said her manager. "You're proving to be a master at allocating just the right resources and guiding them to do what makes your clients happy. Keep it up. That's exactly what I hoped to see when bringing you on board."

Tanya was both delighted and crushed. Impressing her manager was exactly what she hoped to achieve. She also knew that she could not continue to be both sales and technical staff member. However, she accepted the compliments and left her manager's office.

When the architect returned to work, the management team sent him on an assignment out of Tanya's sales district, partially because they believed that Tanya was effectively utilizing her existing technical staff. Tanya pressed on, accepting the plaudits and getting a couple of nice bonuses.

A year passed, and the workload was taking its toll. Tanya's intelligent disobedience impressed her managers and clients, but her health was declining. She had stopped exercising, was drinking to relieve stress, and experienced episodes of anxiety. Although she still loved her job, she quit because she couldn't maintain her approach to delivering outcomes.

Tanya recognizes now that she had allowed her intelligent disobedience, which was supposed to be an exception, to become what was expected by her management team. Her enthusiasm had overshadowed her rationality. She had an exaggerated need to display her competence. When something out of the ordinary was recognized as her strength, her desire to demonstrate keen abilities shut down her truth-sharing and rational approach to her job. Says Tanya now: "You are the only person who can defend your personal time and health. Work will take whatever you give. Your company may appreciate your efforts, but it cannot give your health or family time back to you."

> **You are the only person who can defend your personal time and health.**

One too many failures

In Chapter 2, I discussed regrets about taking action when I knew that the initiative I had been asked to lead presented obstacles. I've also learned from a situation in which I was too patient and did *not* act when I should have.

I was managing 18 logistics experts, coordinating international product shipments between the United States and numerous countries. It was a complicated process to manage, with export/import regulations, substantial paperwork, and widely varying worldwide import tariffs. People with thorough knowledge of this environment are rare. So, when Shane told me that he needed a major change, I was concerned. Shane was a long-term member of the department, with expertise in the business side of international trade. Shane wanted to switch to the technical product analysis area, not leave the department. Shane was a respected colleague, with valuable expertise, so I and other department members were happy to advocate for the change.

Shane started working on the technical side of the department. He asked good questions and designed process change proposals that worked well. After a few weeks, he gained confidence and increased the magnitude of the changes he proposed. A couple of his proposals introduced potential tariff savings, but also introduced risk, because differences in shipping practices might trigger the attention of customs services auditors.

The risks that Shane took made me skeptical. His business savvy led me to protect him when his ideas did not turn out well. Shane was producing both positive and negative outcomes, so I decided to be patient and let him fail. I hoped that would accelerate learning.

However, failures did not temper Shane's proposals; instead, he did less research and proposed process changes that introduced *more* risk. He resembled a gambler trying desperately to recoup his losses. I tried to convince Shane that he did not have to hit a home run with every proposal; rather, he needed to explore possible outcomes more carefully. After another unfortunate outcome, my manager and two employees from my department shared concerns about Shane. They said that he wasn't displaying the right analytical approach and should be returned to his former responsibilities. They were right: I had waited too long to make that change.

From this experience, I learned the following lessons.

- My analysis had been clouded by emotion. I'd hoped that Shane would do well – and I'd let that hope blind me to Shane's lack of progress.
- Past performance of an individual or any act of intelligent disobedience does not guarantee future outcomes. Prior instances of letting others fail for the sake of learning had gone well. I'd relied on that past experience too heavily and did not appropriately watch how it was working with Shane.

> " *Past performance of an individual or any act of intelligent disobedience does not guarantee future outcomes.* "

Oops, he did it again!

Al learned an important lesson about understanding management's tolerance of rule breaking when he was fired for insubordination by repeatedly violating a closely held process.

Al worked for a defense contractor. International business trips were closely scrutinized, especially when confidential design data was carried in a briefcase or on a computer. Both the expense and risk of information loss were closely reviewed. The chief financial officer (CFO) and head of corporate security were briefed regarding any proposed travel, and they would then decide whether to authorize an overseas trip.

Five months before his dismissal, Al had to endorse an overseas trip for one of his employees. The head of corporate security was out to arrange a family funeral. Al received authorization from the CFO, contingent on the approval of the security executive. Al felt strongly about the need for the trip abroad: one of his staff members was uniquely qualified to solve a pressing issue for a customer in the Middle East and timing was of the essence. Al believed that his employee could solve the problem and would also improve the chance of increased revenue from the client. Based on all of these factors, Al made his employee's trip arrangements with his own signature, so that nobody else would experience scrutiny from initiating an international trip without the approval of the head of security.

Al's approval of the trip became a major issue. Multiple interviews examined the basis for his decision and why he believed he had the authority to make that decision. His background in international policy and his understanding of the latest security alerts were also scrutinized. After his time under the microscope, Al kept his job. However, he was told under no circumstances to act in this manner again.

Al felt vindicated when the company was boosted by an expansion of the order from its customer in the Middle East. He was certain that his employee's presence onsite was a factor in the customer's investment decision. Al noticed that none of his management team made mention of his travel approval and whether it was a factor in the customer's procurement decision.

Al faced a similar circumstance five months later. His company's quarterly revenue targets looked unachievable as it neared the end of the fiscal period. Al was in several revenue-focused discussions with senior management when a customer called with a problem that Al could solve. The need for an international trip surfaced, and, this time, both mandatory senior approvers were unavailable. He knew one of the key customer contacts from a prior work assignment. He thought that he could fix their problem and generate the additional revenue that his company so desperately needed. He booked his own ticket and took the trip himself, leaving a message with both senior leaders.

Al solved the customer's problem. They did make a commitment for an order, although the revenue was not quite enough to reach Al's company revenue goal. Upon his return, Al received a voicemail instructing him not to come back to work.

A full investigation of his conduct was being held, and he would be informed of the outcome.

Al lost his job.

In hindsight, Al believes that there were significant inconsistencies between the "do anything for revenue" discussions and the inability to travel to generate that revenue. As Al describes it:

> I poked the bull [senior leadership] five months earlier, and the bull threatened to charge. I poked the bull again, in the same spot, without sufficient support. The bull charged this time and I lost. In the future, I need to ensure that I understand the priorities of direction and constraints provided by management. I will confirm my understanding or propose my own understanding for validation before I act.

" I will confirm my understanding or propose my own understanding for validation before I act. "

Conclusion

These stories demonstrate that no guarantees exist when you engage in intelligent disobedience. However, the negative outcomes in these stories could have been avoided: taking time to reflect on ideas for action and reviewing them with others prior to engaging would have changed the outcomes.

It is important to do your homework, to review your intent with people who may be affected by your actions, and to understand the limits of intelligent disobedience for your organization and your manager before you proceed. Communicating with your manager regarding any actions you take is crucial. Be bold when you can. When acting with intelligent disobedience, ensure that you, your team, and your manager maintain balance, by sharing what you are doing.

Chapter 11

Learning from successful intelligent disobedience

There are many ways in which to approach intelligent disobedience. In addition to the principles and stories shared throughout this book, some approaches are worth noting for their unique circumstances or application. To expand your perspective on the possibilities for utilizing intelligent disobedience, this chapter offers stories that represent different views on duties and ethics, assessing risk before acting, and motivators to achieve desired outcomes.

Being authentic to your higher purpose

Janice is a senior program administrator for a large health management organization (HMO). Her role in the HMO is to design programs for maintaining wellness and preventing illness. She frequently has to balance:

- the demands of designing programs to create positive health outcomes for HMO members;
- the short-term costs of implementing these programs;
- the long-term costs of managing chronic illnesses that may be preventable.

While these three factors can be balanced successfully, programs with high short-term costs challenge managers who have to juggle both short- and long-term financial targets. Because of Janice's substantial role in wellness program design, she is often in the middle of debates regarding these short- and long-term objectives.

Janice is personable, sensitive to the needs and moods of others, and well respected in the organization. That does not mean that she's a pushover: she will battle long and hard for what she believes in, including executing intelligent disobedience, when required. Her approach often isn't subtle. She once proclaimed, in an open session, "Co-design with members in this organization is a joke."

Challenging the HMO's chief financial officer in a way that triggers his greatest concerns is not out of the question for Janice, when doing so surfaces a truth that must be confronted. Persistence is another of her successful tools, such as repeating "This simply isn't good enough" during negotiations. She does this to ensure that her peers do not give up on finding common ground to help to achieve good outcomes for HMO members and the HMO's financial targets.

How is Janice able to be so direct, to challenge others in open sessions, and yet still maintain the respect of her peers? She attributes her success to two factors: her assessment of actions against her higher purpose, and building relationships based on trust.

Janice's higher-purpose assessment

Before engaging in intelligent disobedience or challenging others in her organization, Janice asks herself the following questions.

- Am I certain I want to do this?
- Why is this important?
- Do I have a clear view of the outcome?
- Am I arguing based on ego, because I need to be right or seek to be valued or perceived as belonging to a group within my organization?
- Am I doing this for the benefit of others, without sacrificing my authentic self in the process?
- Is my approach the only approach that would work?
- Do I fully understand the intent and motivations of others involved in this decision?
- Does my idea for intelligent disobedience embrace the *intent* of existing processes and guidelines, even if it does not follow them?
- Is this situation an accumulation of prior faulty decisions, or will this decision set a precedent for good (or bad) decisions in the future?
- Will staying quiet represent a value mismatch between the role I serve for members and my need to support the HMO's objectives?
- Am I ready to apologize if I get this wrong?

Janice's trust-based relationships

According to Janice, trust-based relationships require self-work. While her role is intended to provide benefits to others, she conveys a keen concern to not sacrifice herself:

> *You can't be trusted by others if you can't like yourself, trust yourself, and be true to your higher purpose.*

You can't be trusted by others if you can't like yourself, trust yourself, and be true to your higher purpose. If you focus your energy on appropriate intentions, ensure your ego is not driving your actions or statements, follow through to the finish, and achieve your objectives, the trust will follow.

The trust that Janice has developed allows her to be direct and also, on rare occasion, to express anger when the stakes are high and decisions are not being made. Furthermore, that trust allows her the latitude to move forward with new ideas, even if she has only partial information. Similar to the consideration for intuition discussed in Chapter 5, Janice can move forward with initiatives before she has all of the answers that her management team requires. Her track record on following through and being thorough with analysis of HMO and member outcomes has given her considerable latitude to act. She can extend her activities beyond her role, forge ahead without working out details up front, and challenge her colleagues, both in private and open settings.

Some items worth noting about Janice and her approach are as follows.

- She does not assess risk to her career when considering intelligent disobedience; rather, she focuses on whether it supports her higher purpose and will provide positive business outcomes. In her view, silence when appropriate outcomes could be at risk is out of the question: that would not support her "higher purpose."

- She will not sacrifice herself – that is, her personal well-being, balance, and personal health – for the sake of engaging in intelligent disobedience or pushing back against management. She evaluates the pace of change and her ability to address it before taking action. She also has refused several promotions to maintain balance between making a difference and being true to herself and her higher purpose.

Refuse a direction and discover truth

Greg is a project manager for a training organization. His responsibility is to oversee training, from the initiation of a training idea or client request through to measuring the effectiveness of training outcomes. In this role, he works with a variety of clients who have varying levels of experience with designing and integrating training into their business environment. One of his less sophisticated clients presented an interesting issue.

Greg was leading an important and high-visibility initiative to increase the capability and effectiveness of a large group of project managers in a national non-profit organization. The organization had just streamlined its project management processes. Greg's objective was to design and coordinate the delivery of training to teach the project managers about the new processes and to enhance their ability to work as internal consultants within their own organization. To implement the processes as quickly as possible, the engagement was ambitious: 600 people trained in seven weeks. As an additional challenge, Greg's sponsor and a peer manager in the client organization had differing views about the approach that the training should take, so Greg had to monitor their perceptions carefully.

To ensure that the training materials were effective for attendees and to help to resolve the managers' difference of opinion, they held a pilot education session with 22 participants from various departments. The initial feedback was quite positive, so the training sessions for 600 people were scheduled around the country over the course of the seven weeks.

Then Greg got a phone call from his client sponsor.

The sponsor had received unfavorable feedback from the pilot session – contradictory to the initial verbal feedback– and he wanted the training sessions cancelled. Greg agreed and said that he would come to the sponsor's office immediately. That was when his acts of intelligent disobedience started. He did not cancel any of the sessions; instead, he had the instructors ask their attendees about any feedback they had heard from the pilot. From the instructors' responses and his own discussions within his client's organization, he quickly determined that the unfavorable feedback came from a single person who reported to the skeptical peer manager. The skeptical manager, in turn, expressed doubt about the training to his manager, who was also the sponsor's senior executive. Greg and his training initiative were caught in the middle of a political battle between two high-level managers, one of whom had got a senior vice president involved.

Greg did not discuss ways of salvaging the training program with his sponsor or point a finger at managers in his client's organization. He did not want to get any farther into the political battle – especially because only one of the attendees had an issue, and the feedback was likely filtered and exaggerated by the skeptical manager. In addition, Greg did not want to embarrass his sponsor. He was tempted to tell his sponsor that he was pulling the plug on the training program prematurely without understanding what was going on – but he took a different approach. In Greg's words: "I did not want to weaponize the information against my sponsor. Instead, I tried to generate a learning moment."

Greg told the sponsor that the sponsor's peer manager might be trying to "parlay a political move" on him and that he should respond to the challenge. The sponsor decided to collect detailed information from all of the pilot session attendees. Greg offered to help at no charge, to protect his sponsor. From his research, Greg was certain that the skeptical peer manager was trying to save face because the pilot had gone so well.

The detailed data collected from the pilot participants reinforced the initial feedback: the training was effective and well delivered. The skeptical peer manager was silenced when the senior vice president heard the full details of the feedback and where the negative input originated. The training was completed and was declared "the strongest training program ever delivered within the organization."

The following are the notable intelligent disobedience activities that Greg used in this situation.

- He ignored the direction he was given to cancel the training events. In fact, he directly countered the direction by asking the facilitators to collect information to prepare themselves for the training, while also obtaining valuable information about the negative feedback.
- Greg worked to support the sponsor within his organization, rather than to defend the training program and pilot results. Instead of using data as leverage against someone, he applied it to support his sponsor, which, in turn, helped his client and Greg's initiative.
- His actions embraced the premise that no single person owns the truth in an organization; everyone involved owns a bit of truth (see Chapter 7). Putting that pool of truth on the table solidified the position of the training sponsor and Greg's training program.
- Greg shared that "he did not even think" of risks to his program or his career when he acted with intelligent disobedience and didn't cancel the training. He did, however, perform a risk assessment: he assessed risks to his relationship with his sponsor. He accurately deduced that the training program would be successful if he could support and solidify his sponsor's position. In addition, the successful training program would bolster Greg's stance within his own company.

Trust and the chess master

Dottie is an executive in a technology services outsourcing company. She provides managerial oversight for many clients in the travel and transportation industry, which includes monitoring the services provided, ensuring that contracted performance and response time levels are maintained, and the allocation and coordination of staff members distributed throughout the world. Her objectives are to ensure that her client's business needs are met, to deliver on schedule to her clients, to deliver against profit and cost-savings targets, and to ensure that her staff members are utilized efficiently and effectively. It's a hectic job and Dottie's management team scrutinizes the measurements she is accountable for.

To manage costs, it's important for Dottie to manage the scope of work provided to her clients. Some clients are not familiar with the details of their outsourcing contracts, so Dottie carefully reviews the scope of services delivered. The outsourcing services contracts do not always fully anticipate changing client needs, which her teams must manage. She often receives client requests reflecting those changing needs, requiring her to decide between incurring extra cost and satisfying the client. This adds a dimension to managing her geographically dispersed skilled staff. This intricate set of interconnected elements often requires quick decisions that Dottie cannot review with her remotely located management team.

When she receives a legitimate out-of-scope client request, Dottie has two decisions to make. First, does she provide those out-of-scope services? Second, does she do that for a fee or for free (as a gesture of goodwill to potentially sell services in the future)? She has neither the extra budget for out-of-scope opportunities nor the authority to provide out-of-scope service in any circumstance.

How does she manage this balancing act? Dottie says that three things are pivotal in this situation: playing chess by knowing that multiple moves win the game, knowing when to share and not to share her moves with her management team, and having a healthy fear of failure.

Playing chess

Dottie does not look at a single out-of-scope delivery as an individual act of intelligent disobedience; rather, she seeks opportunities to reallocate funding or to reassign a staff member to trigger a series of activities that benefit her clients and meet her team's needs. When taking action, Dottie also considers which activities her management team monitors.

Dottie shares this example:

> I once posted a job for a skill that was held in high regard as opposed to the skill my team needed. After I hired the person with the skills I actually needed (versus the skills listed in the job posting), I moved that person to two different accounts for a couple of months, had him cover for a staff member who needed surgery, then placed him permanently on an account where we signed a deal to provide expanded services that required his skills.

> What I do is play chess. I look several moves ahead, rather than view things as a single problem to solve or disobedience that I need to justify. I consider what I need holistically, for several clients over a few months to a year in the future. I "sneak in" resources and/or shift funding around to get what I need.

Dottie maintains insurance for her intelligent disobedience by shifting resources or funding with her peers in other industries. This is important, because she admits that she sometimes makes mistakes in her chess playing – but by keeping communication open with her peers, she rarely gets caught out. She engages in intelligent disobedience through nonstandard hiring approaches or shifting funds between client accounts. She considers multiple sets of chess moves before she provides any out-of-scope service to prevent impacts to her performance targets.

Knowing when to share

Dottie's management team leaves her alone because she gets the results they seek. According to Dottie, she is viewed as creative, rather than disobedient. This perspective comes about after the fact, when she hits a financial target or adds people to an account and management asks, "How did you do that?" She then explains the steps she took – some against the rules – to get the desired outcome. At times, she does feel the need to alert her management team. It is "mostly gut feel" about when to do this, says Dottie, but her intuition is enhanced by her understanding of what makes her management team nervous. Nervous managers ask more questions, which could hamper her flexibility and rule breaking. So, in advance, she communicates her confidence in solving a problem or some of the steps that she intends to take. This normally relieves the tension and allows Dottie to utilize the intelligent disobedience creativity she needs to accomplish her goals.

> *" intuition is enhanced by her understanding of what makes her management team nervous. "*

Healthy fear of failure

Dottie rarely assesses risk in terms such as, "What if I get caught cheating?" Her primary risk assessment is of the outcome she desires. She feels compelled to meet her targets and to deliver the right products for her clients, while satisfying the requirements of her management team. Doing the "*right* thing," says Dottie, is what her management team believes is appropriate:

> The *best* thing, however, is what will yield the best outcome for clients and my business. Figuring out how to do the best thing, rather than the right thing, is what keeps me up at night. I am much more worried about not delivering the best thing than I am getting in trouble for breaking the rules. I am healthy when I worry about delivering service, but would be a wreck if I had to worry about obeying all of the rules and following every procedure.

Sometimes the witness should *not* "just answer the question!"

Nadine works in a government agency that is modernizing processes to accommodate the wider variety of community desires brought about by cultural changes, security requirements, and shifts in government priorities. She oversees a series of initiatives focused on pushing leadership down the organization chart, which, while philosophically embraced by the management team, has proven difficult to accomplish. Old habits – especially deferring responsibility to a higher authority – remain strongly held.

Nadine was already running four change initiatives that were struggling with these old habits when a senior official asked her to prepare a brief for review with a legislative panel. The brief would propose streamlined procurement practices in special circumstances – particularly where security or hardship needs are evident. Under these circumstances, procurement authority would be pushed lower in the organizational hierarchy to allow for greater agility and responsiveness. The idea was fundamentally sound. However, Nadine was certain that the organization wasn't ready for this change, given its resistance to other changes that distributed authority and because the requested brief took distribution of authority a step farther, to the expenditure of funds.

The requested brief was within Nadine's scope of responsibility, and she felt confident she could put together a document that spelled out the "right" steps. However, she also believed the brief would lead to a change initiative that could not be delivered, no matter how many caveats she included in the document. Because she could not ignore the request, she decided to engage in intelligent disobedience and temporarily evade the question.

Rather than draft the brief, Nadine launched a series of queries, putting the premise of the presumed outcomes in question. Preparedness and definitions of the situations under which the procurement authority would be distributed was questioned, as well as the procurement concept's relationships with other struggling initiatives. Nadine knew that the questions would not be easy to answer and that her manager would likely turn the questions back to her to resolve. In short, she nominated herself as temporary blocker for the initiative. She bought herself time in which to perform analysis.

To perform her analysis, Nadine talked with department heads about the concerns they had and the clarity they would need to execute new procurement powers. As she expected, there was wide disagreement, leading to significant arguments that clearly highlighted the organization's lack of readiness for the change. These specific arguments and concerns with the sources listed were relayed to the senior official who requested the brief. They validated and expanded Nadine's concern, without her being the blocker of the initiative, which her senior managers would have viewed unfavorably. The collective concerns upheld and expanded her point, so appropriate analysis could be performed to determine whether a reduced form of the procurement initiative could be implemented in the short term.

After a full analysis was performed, a significantly limited scope of the procurement initiative was implemented. Outcomes from this were positive and served as a proof of concept for other areas of the agency to mimic. A slower adoption of the overall premise was the result, with positive outcomes.

Two items of note from Nadine's story are as follows.

- While normally an enabler for change, Nadine found it necessary to block an initiative that was ill-timed and doomed to failure – much like Chap, the seeing-eye dog who leapt in front of the defective elevator, whom we met in the Introduction. Blocking averted the issue and also presented risk if Nadine did not follow up. Nadine used the time to refine and gather more detailed information to substantiate her position. She shifted the source of the concerns from herself to the managers who were struggling with the magnitude of change in the organization. Once again, collecting truth for view by multiple individuals is an effective technique to substantiate intelligent disobedience.
- Nadine believed that the value from the procurement change idea could be leveraged under the right circumstances. Through continued probing, she defined pockets within her organization that would accept the responsibility of managing procurement. Persistence can be a fundamental element of intelligent disobedience; Nadine's activities to embrace a valid idea and find areas in which that idea could be adopted is an example of effectively using persistence.

Support curiosity, convey confidence, and embrace modesty

In Chapter 2, we heard about Stephan, who had successfully pushed back against his senior officers at the Pentagon by volunteering additional information and being mindful of the challenges they face while making decisions. Stephan embraces three characteristics in his approach to work.

- He believes that his truth is valid and worth discussing, and he is constantly aware that the truth others bring to the table could be drastically different from his own. He openly seeks that truth with genuine curiosity and care for the welfare of the people in his organization. His almost childlike curiosity is a powerful catalyst for openness and truth telling among his peers, resulting in better solutions being proposed.

- Stephan also conveys confidence, but not in his abilities when working alone. He generates great confidence from teams he assembles, in part because he's so effective at being a catalyst for ideas to be aired for discussion. Stephan attributes his success to his teams and conveys that success to others whenever he can. People want to work with Stephan. They dedicate themselves to success when Stephan is at the helm.

- Stephan is disarmingly modest. He rarely takes credit for successes, and although he has considerable skills, he never discusses his personal strengths. He uses a keen sense of understanding others to form the teams he leads, and he readily sees the value of what is possible with dedication and focus. While not a common characteristic of people who are adept at managing with intelligent disobedience, Stephan uses his modesty effectively. Combined with the ability to draw ideas and truth out of others and an insatiable optimism to gain opportunities others can't, he is extremely successful.

Stephan' story is not about an event, but a progressive set of opportunities that his particular approach to intelligent disobedience has generated. In 15 years, Stephan has grown from a project manager to a program manager, to a government department director handling large disaster relief efforts, to a director for a defense industry firm, to vice president of a multinational manufacturing company known for its innovation. His intelligent disobedience is the atypical way in which he applies his strengths to achieve outstanding results.

Conclusion

People who successfully engage in intelligent disobedience rely on significantly different approaches and are driven by varying perceptions of risk. From the more holistic "in service to a higher purpose" to a very emotional fear of failure in the longer term, people view risk quite differently. These are all valid, suiting the profile of each individual. Understanding the environments in which they work and evaluating the needs and strengths of people around them are other characteristics shared by the people highlighted in these stories. Their ability to listen, to understand others, and to act with confidence are keenly refined, which ensures that their acts of intelligent disobedience are successful.

> " People who successfully engage in intelligent disobedience rely on significantly different approaches and are driven by varying perceptions of risk. "

Chapter 12

A call to action
The next step is yours

While most acts of intelligent disobedience are performed alone, you don't have to navigate these potentially turbulent waters by yourself. You can collaborate with senior leaders and peers to discuss potential acts of intelligent disobedience, formulate approaches for homework to help you to ensure success, and rehearse your 30-second stories and 30-minute discussions. Here are some available resources you can access today.

Online resources

The Intelligent Disobedience Leadership website, http://www.intelligentdis obedience.com, offers abundant resources, including links to intelligent disobedience events and to an intelligent disobedience presentation in the LinkedIn Learning online library. In addition, the site has a blog, where the Intelligent Disobedience Leadership team provides deployment hints and tips, shares new techniques, and tells stories from leaders around the world who embrace this leadership concept. Also, you can contact me at bob@intelligentdisobedience. com. I will strive to respond promptly – especially if you grab my attention with a great 30-second story!

Keynote presentations and workshops

My colleagues and I at Intelligent Disobedience Leadership can help you and your management team to integrate and deploy intelligent disobedience in your organization through keynote presentations and highly interactive on-site workshops. You can join companies in North America, Europe, Asia, Australia, and New Zealand that have benefited from these energetic and thought-provoking events. All workshops include 10 hours of post-workshop coaching sessions to help you to embed new habits with your teams. Go to http://www.intelligentdisobedience. com/workshops for sample workshop agendas. Contact info@intelligentdisobedi ence.com for more information.

Start a community of practice (CoP)

Setting up a community of practice (CoP) in your workplace helps employees to refine and use intelligent disobedience techniques effectively. Intelligent disobedience is contextual; it requires tailoring to your environment and organizational culture, and the styles of your leadership team. The skills profile of teams you lead may also require adjustment to fully capitalize on the power of intelligent disobedience. The tools and approaches discussed in this book are a starting point, serving as a catalyst for outcome improvement. Having regular discussions with your peers, managers, and team members, sharing experiences regarding your workplace and clients, and refining your approaches to intelligent disobedience will escalate your success.

A CoP engages in monthly discussions about intelligent disobedience. One recommendation is to pick a tool from the book – such as the Intelligent Disobedience Decision Model in Chapter 5 or the conditions for truth-telling in Chapter 7 – and customize it for your organization. After deploying the revised tool for a few months, re-evaluate it and fine-tune it, if required. You might also present scenarios to your group and discuss potential acts of intelligent disobedience that could be deployed – or whether intelligent disobedience is a good idea at all, given the circumstances.

For help launching and running your own CoP, send an email to info@intelligentdisobedience.com and request a free starter kit. The kit includes an intelligent disobedience CoP intent and objectives guide, a draft letter you can use to invite attendees to your first meeting, and sample meeting agendas.

Coaching

Coaching is available for one-on-one or group sessions to hone your intelligent disobedience approaches and techniques. After you've had a chance to practice intelligent disobedience, coaching is an effective way of taking this leadership skill to the next level. Contact info@intelligentdisobedience.com and we will create a coaching package to suit your needs.

Let's get social!

Join an ongoing dialog on intelligent disobedience! You can reach us on Facebook by liking Intelligent Disobedience Leadership, join the Intelligent Disobedience Leadership LinkedIn page, or follow me on Twitter (@bobmcgannon) or on LinkedIn (Bob McGannon).

Goodbye . . . for now

I hope you have enjoyed this book as the start (or continuation!) of a long and fruitful practice of intelligent disobedience. I believe it is an elevated moral, ethical, and high-performance approach to adding value to our business, client, and personal lives. Applying our truths with balance and confidence, and embracing our colleagues' truths, will lead to better outcomes, fewer regrets, and greater degrees of personal authenticity.

Index

Note: Pages in bold refer to text within tables, and pages in italics refer to text within figures.